THE HAPPY ADOPTED DOG

Tammy Gagne

The Happy Adopted Dog

Project Team
Editor: Mary E. Grangeia
Copy Editor: Joann Woy
Indexer: Elizabeth Walker
Design: Patricia Escabi
Series Design: Stephanie Krautheim and Mada Design
Series Originator: Dominique De Vito

T.F.H. Publications
President/CEO: Glen S. Axelrod
Executive Vice President: Mark E. Johnson
Publisher: Christopher T. Reggio
Production Manager: Kathy Bontz

T.F.H. Publications, Inc.
One TFH Plaza
Third and Union Avenues
Neptune City, NJ 07753

Printed and bound in China
09 10 11 12 13   3 5 7 9 8 6 4 2

Library of Congress Cataloging-in-Publication Data
Gagne, Tammy.
  The happy adopted dog : how to adopt the perfect family dog / Tammy Gagne.
      p. cm.
  Includes bibliographical references and index.
  ISBN 978-0-7938-3687-1 (alk. paper)
 1. Dogs. I. Title.
 SF426.G34 2009
 636.7—dc22
                                    2009004333

This book has been published with the intent to provide accurate and authoritative information in regard to the subject matter within. While every reasonable precaution has been taken in preparation of this book, the author and publisher expressly disclaim responsibility for any errors, omissions, or adverse effects arising from the use or application of the information contained herein. The techniques and suggestions are used at the reader's discretion and are not to be considered a substitute for veterinary care. If you suspect a medical problem consult your veterinarian.

The Leader In Responsible Animal Care For Over 50 Years!®
www.tfh.com

TABLE OF CONTENTS

1

WHY

Adopt a Dog?

I f you are thinking about adopting a dog, there has never been a better time. According to the Humane Society of the United States (HSUS), six to eight million dogs and cats enter shelters each year. Of these animals, between three and four million are euthanized because there aren't enough owners to adopt them all. By adopting a dog, you play an important role in changing these statistics. Every dog adopted from a shelter is one less euthanized animal.

AREN'T ALL DOGS ADOPTED?

Many pet owners think of their beloved dogs as being adopted, even if they purchased them from breeders or pet stores. After all, these loving owners chose their amazing animals and welcomed them into their homes as new members of their families. While all dogs may be thought of as adopted family members, dog adoption has a very different meaning to people involved in the process of rehoming animals in shelters and breed rescues. To these individuals, adoption means giving a dog a vital second chance at life.

Adopting, or rescuing, a dog means to welcome him into your home and family after he has been relinquished to a shelter or breed rescue by a previous owner. The reasons dogs are surrendered can vary significantly from one situation to another, but all of these animals share a common predicament. Each one desperately needs a responsible person to love and care for him.

THE BENEFITS OF ADOPTION

By adopting a dog, you are approaching pet ownership in both a humane and socially responsible way. But adoption is not a matter of sacrifice or settling. Adoption offers countless advantages to dog owners. Most adoptive owners get just as much from their relationships with their dogs as they give. In fact, the more owners put into dog ownership, the more they usually get back from their adopted pets. Many owners consider adoption to be one of the most rewarding experiences of their lives.

By adopting a dog, you give him a vital second chance at life.

Making a Difference

The most profound reward of adoption is the feeling an owner gets from knowing that he or she has helped saved a life. Sadly, the majority of animals who are not adopted from shelters within a certain time period are euthanized. By adopting a dog, you not only help an animal by giving him a home, but you also help your community. With the number of animals languishing in shelters across the United States well into the millions, each and every person who chooses to adopt is helping solve the gargantuan problem of unwanted and homeless pets.

Owners who adopt also play an important role in ending the suffering of puppy mill dogs. Puppies bred by these breeding facilities spend the first few weeks of their lives in cages piled several high. They are not exercised or socialized, and they are forced to eat and sleep in crowded conditions. Still, the puppies are the luckier ones because they are able to leave once they are old enough to be sold. The parents of these young dogs, however, spend their entire lives in this unpleasant environment. When more people adopt, the demand for puppy mill dogs drops. Making the puppy mill business less lucrative is our best means of lessening the number of breeders who churn out animals purely for profit.

Smart Investments of Time and Money

There are less altruistic (yet still significant) benefits to adoption as well. Puppies, both purebreds and so-called designer breed mixes, can be extremely expensive to buy. Adopting a dog generally entails a nominal fee to cover the cost of feeding and spaying or neutering the dog. But even this fee pales in comparison to the cost of buying a dog from a breeder or pet store. Adoption should never be looked at as a means of finding a bargain, however. You may pay considerably less for a shelter or rescue dog up front, but this is where the savings end. Once you bring him home, your adopted dog will need all the same things as a dog with a higher price tag.

One thing owners do save by adopting a dog is energy. While young puppies are certainly adorable, they are also extremely demanding. The task that most puppy owners dread the most— housetraining— is already behind most adult dogs. Even young puppies kept in foster care before being placed with permanent caregivers are usually partially or fully housetrained by the time they go home with their new families. Another challenge of puppyhood— teething— is also a thing of the past for many dogs by the time of adoption.

Most puppies have seemingly endless vigor. If you are an older adult, or simply lack the stamina to keep up with a younger dog, adopting an older pet may suit your lifestyle much better than buying a puppy. Young professionals also often make great matches for older dogs because these more mature pets require less training and constant supervision than their younger counterparts.

Get an Animal for Life

A good number of the homeless animals living in shelters are puppies and kittens, victims of irresponsible people who allowed their pets to breed. But there are at least as many dogs and cats at the shelter who are more than a year old—animals who were obtained by people who didn't think through the responsibilities of pet ownership before they got them.

Please, don't make the same mistake. Think before you adopt. Sharing your life with a companion animal can bring incredible rewards, but only if you're willing to make the necessary commitments of time, money, responsibility, and love for the life of the pet.

(Courtesy of the Humane Society of the United States)

Broad Selection of Ages and Types

If you have your heart set on a purebred dog, you may wonder if adopting means compromising on this point. Thankfully, this isn't the case. According to the HSUS, about a third of the dogs in the nation's animal shelters are indeed purebreds. If you have any trouble finding a particular breed at a shelter, check with your local breed rescue group. These regional organizations specialize in placing dogs of specific breeds.

Hundreds of different dog breeds exist, each with its own unique set of characteristics. From large dogs like the German Shepherd and medium-sized breeds like Dalmatian to tiny dogs like the Papillon, there is a breed to suit virtually any pet lover. Do you prefer an active animal who basks in being outdoors? If so, a Siberian Husky may be right for you. If instead you'd like a dog who prefers cuddling to calisthenics, a Japanese Chin may be out there just waiting for you to find him.

For people who prefer mixed breeds, there are plenty of adoptees to go around as well. Dogs of mixed lineage, commonly called mutts, offer their own special perks. Mixed breeds combine the various qualities of different purebreds. Many owners of these "Heinz 57" varieties insist that mixed breeds have better temperaments than some purebreds. Mutts also tend to be less prone to numerous health problems that plague a vast number of purebreds.

Dogs in shelters and breed rescues also come in a wide variety of ages. People often assume that all dogs in need of adoption are older animals, but many are actually quite young. The average age of a dog in a breed rescue, for example, is just three years old. Puppies and young adult dogs enter shelters and rescue groups each day, and they need new homes just as much as their elder equivalents. The very thing that makes the unwanted pet population the enormous problem that it is, with millions of dogs in need of new homes, is the reason adoptive owners have such a large selection.

THE DOWNSIDE TO ADOPTION

For all its benefits, adoption also has its undeniable disadvantages. To paint an inviting picture of adoption without acknowledging these legitimate drawbacks would be irresponsible. Adoption is not for everyone. In fact, if adoption isn't right for you, you won't do anyone any favors—not yourself and certainly not the dog whose care you assume.

For a long time it was unfairly assumed that all adopted dogs came with problem behaviors. Fortunately, this stereotype has been largely erased in recent decades. Countless success stories have helped to change the average dog owner's perspective about giving a previously-homed pet a second (or even third or fourth) chance. In fact, adopting a dog from a shelter or from a breed rescue has become the most socially acceptable way of finding a pet. Prospective adoptive owners must realize, however, that adoption requires the same level of research and scrutiny as buying a dog from a breeder. The sad fact is that many dogs available for adoption do come with some unpleasant baggage.

Abuse, Neglect, or Good Intentions Gone Wrong

Sometimes purebred dogs are acquired for incredibly superficial reasons. Perhaps someone decides they want to own a breed just like the one they saw in a movie or on television, or

Dogs in shelters and breed rescues come in a wide variety of types and ages.

maybe they want a member of the breed that won the Westminster Dog Show. Some owners seek dogs they think will enhance their own image. For example, some people erroneously equate large, intimidating breeds with masculinity, while others seem to think toy breeds are the quintessential fashion accessory. The reasons can be as different as the people themselves, but if an owner doesn't know what he or she is getting into before buying a dog, the chances are far greater that the animal will end up in need of being rehomed down the road. Owners who cannot bother themselves with doing their homework before buying a dog usually don't make the time and effort necessary to train their dogs either. This lack of commitment on behalf of impetuous owners leaves as many dogs in need of retraining as they are in need of people who care enough about them to follow through with what their previous owners did not.

Some owners buy (or adopt) dogs with the best intentions, only to realize later that they have bitten off far more than they can chew. This is usually a result of poor breed selection or a bad match of a specific dog with an owner. In some ways the damage done by these well-meaning original owners is even greater than that done by less caring individuals. These owners love their dogs, so it usually takes much longer for them to admit that they are in over their heads. During this process valuable training time is lost, and bad behaviors often become more deeply ingrained. This makes retraining even more difficult for the dog's next caregiver.

Countless dogs in need of new homes have been neglected or abused at some point in their lives. An overwhelming number of animals end up in shelters whenever authorities raid a puppy mill and remove dogs due to improper care. This does not mean these dogs cannot make good pets for the right people, but it does drastically affect the pool from which their potential owners can be drawn. For instance, a dog who has been abused by a man may shy away from other human males. Pets who have been abused in the past need to be treated with a significant amount of patience. It can be frustrating for an owner who wants to be lavished with canine kisses to wait for his or her adopted pet to begin to trust again.

Unknown Histories

The volunteers who handle intake for shelters and breed rescues do their best to document each dog's history so that every animal can be placed with the best possible owner. Sometimes, though, it just isn't feasible to get all the relevant information. Even the dog's age may be unknown, although a veterinarian can usually estimate it.

Adopting a dog from a shelter or from a breed rescue has become the most socially acceptable way of finding a pet.

The volunteers also may not know how a dog was treated in his previous home (or homes). In many of these situations the dogs' temperaments are evaluated, and any obvious behavior problems are addressed through training prior to placement. You may never fully know just what your adopted dog endured before he found his permanent home with you. He may exhibit certain behavior problems that suggest he was mistreated, but these behaviors may have a different cause altogether.

Some problems require more work on the part of a new owner than others. Many rescue dogs merely need to learn basic obedience skills or go through a period of remedial housetraining. Other problems are more serious. Separation anxiety, for example,

often necessitates the help of a professional dog trainer. Thankfully, most of the problems that adoptive owners face are manageable, but you must be certain that you are willing and able to deal with the problems that may arise *before* deciding to adopt a dog.

Health Issues

Some dogs in shelters and rescues have been given up because they suffer from health problems. In some of these cases, the dogs' previous owners couldn't afford to provide their pets with the medical treatment they needed. In other cases, the owners simply didn't want to be bothered by a dog with a chronic condition. In either situation the new owner will be responsible for paying for any medications or ongoing treatments that the animal needs.

Even seemingly healthy shelter dogs can end up suffering from a medical problem at some point in their lives. Because so much is often unknown about these animals, there is no way to predict which problems may arise in the future. While you may be tempted to see this as a disadvantage, it is important to remember that even newborn puppies bred by responsible breeders may develop the exact same afflictions as a dog you find at a shelter.

Weighty Issues

When you think of a shelter dog, you may imagine an emaciated animal. While many dogs in need of new homes have indeed been malnourished in the past, obesity is another common problem that shelter dogs face. A good number of dogs arrive at shelters and rescues considerably overweight. While this is almost always a manageable situation, it will require work and dedication on behalf of the new owner. A consultation with a veterinarian is the best way to find out exactly how much weight a

Shelter and breed rescue volunteers work to document each dog's history so that every animal can be placed with the best possible owner.

Is Your Mama a Labrador?

At one time an owner could only guess what his or her mixed breed's lineage might be. Perhaps a dog's ears were unmistakably those of a hound dog and his temperament was totally terrier, but his short, stubby tail was a total mystery. Now, however, those days of supposition and uncertainty are behind us, thanks to a groundbreaking new DNA test that detects 134 AKC-recognized breeds and subsequently reveals an individual dog's genetic makeup. While some owners care little whether their mutt is half Pointer or a quarter Pekingese, others enjoy learning about their dogs' ancestry. Knowing which breeds your dog can call his great-grandparents can even help keep him healthy because this kind of information can assist in predicting which health issues your dog may face during his lifetime.

dog must lose. A vet can also help the new owner plan diet and exercise strategies to help achieve this important goal.

Ch-Ch-Changes

If you adopt a mixed breed, it may be difficult to predict exactly how he will change as he grows older, especially if you do not know which breeds are in his lineage. A young puppy may resemble one parent more than the other, but this can change incredibly quickly. A 5-pound (2-kg) pup can grow into a 50-pound (23-kg) dog in just a matter of months. Other features can change, too, such as markings and hair texture. Thankfully, temperaments are usually more consistent than physical characteristics. If you remain dedicated to training and socializing your dog, he should remain as affable as he was when you met him, if not even more so.

ARE YOU READY TO ADOPT A DOG?

If you think an adopted dog may be right for you, the next step is deciding whether you would make a good adoptive owner. Dogs in need of homes come in a full array of sizes, shapes, and personalities. They can also have drastically different needs. When potential owners do their homework, they can find pets whose needs best match their abilities and lifestyles. Even the best match, however, must come along at the right time in an owner's life.

Examine Your Decision to Adopt

Many people adopt a dog because their kids want a pet or because they want their children to experience the joys and responsibilities of dog ownership. Others adopt because they want to help animals in need. As reasonable as these goals may seem, none of them should be the driving force behind your decision to adopt a pet. You may want to make a difference in the lives of your kids and the animal you chose, but above all else you must want to bring this particular dog into your life.

If your children are extremely young, it may be smart to wait a while before adopting. Kids less than six years of age typically have a hard time understanding the ground rules for how to properly treat a pet. Even the best natured dogs may growl or bite in reaction to having their ears or tails pulled. Larger dogs can inadvertently knock over toddlers or preschoolers. For the safety of all involved, timing is crucial for families considering dog adoption.

Some people want to adopt because their previous pet has passed away and they miss the companionship a dog offers. Or maybe they have an interest in training and wish to enter a dog in obedience trials. Neither of these reasons is better than the other, but there are certain reasons no one should ever use for adopting. If you want a dog to protect your home, for example, a wiser choice would be a security system. Likewise, you shouldn't adopt a dog because adoption seems like the fashionable thing to do. Also, avoid selecting a dog based on appearance alone. You may love the look of a Border Collie, for example, but this breed, like many others, has very specific needs. You must fully understand what caring for a particular dog entails before deciding to adopt him.

Consider Your Circumstances

In addition to carefully selecting a dog for adoption, you must also consider your own personal circumstances. Do you have enough time for a dog at this point in your life? Some adopted dogs need considerably more training (or retraining) than others. Do you work long hours? While a handful of breeds may be able to spend large chunks of time alone without a problem, this scenario is far from ideal. Even if you work normal business hours, can you make it home on your lunch break for a quick

walk? If not, is someone else in your household able to perform this important task? Most dogs need to relieve themselves at least every four to six hours. Does your job require you to travel frequently? If so, who will care for your dog during these times you are away?

Can you afford to care for the breed you have chosen? Bulldogs, for example, tend to need more veterinary care than a lot of other dogs. Larger breeds mean higher food bills. Even a healthy dog needs regular veterinary exams and preventive medicines. Professional training and grooming can also be expensive. If your solution to juggling a dog with a busy work schedule is utilizing doggy daycare, have you factored the cost of this service into your budget?

By doing their homework, most potential adoptive owners can find pets whose needs match their abilities and lifestyles.

You must be willing to fulfill all your dog's needs, even when you are tired or not in the mood. When you arrive home at the end of the day, your dog still needs to be taken to his potty spot, exercised, and fed, and then taken to his potty spot once more. All dogs need daily companionship and stimulation to remain emotionally and mentally content, so you will need to spend some quality time with your pet each day. The good news is that caring for your pet can be a great way of improving your own mood. Going for a walk with your best canine friend can be an excellent way to recharge your own battery or make the day's stressors seem a little less important.

When you consider kicking back at home with your new pet, remember your home will be your dog's new home. How will this work? Many apartment buildings and condominiums allow dogs, but some have very specific requirements relating to breed and size. Even if you are certain your landlord or management

Setting Reasonable Limits

Many of us wish we could adopt all the dogs we see at our local animal shelters, but if we truly want to help them, we must be realistic. Overextending—be it with your time or your financial resources—won't do anything to help animals in need of new homes. On the contrary, making unrealistic commitments can actually hurt the animals you want to help. Even the most committed pet owner can only properly care for a few animals at a time. Spreading yourself too thin can result in neglect and unnecessary stress for all involved. Additionally, some dogs function best in homes in which they are the only pets. If a dog has special needs, be certain you are prepared to deal with his specific issues. In some situations, a willingness to learn isn't enough. Some dogs need owners with considerable training experience. Being sensible in deciding which and how many dogs you can handle is the first step in making a positive difference.

company allows pets, be sure to get it in writing. The worst time to find out that a policy has changed is after you have already adopted your new dog.

Be sure your home environment complements the breed you choose. Alaskan Malamutes, for instance, are a poor choice for apartment dwellers because they delight in being outdoors, even in the coldest weather. Retired Greyhounds surprisingly do not need as much exercise as people suspect, but these sighthounds cannot resist the temptation to chase a passing squirrel, so they need high fences in their backyards or they must be leashed whenever outdoors.

Aside from time and money, you must also consider whether you have sufficient knowledge of and experience with the type of dog you wish to adopt. A 20-pound (9-kg) Poodle mix whose owners moved to an apartment building that didn't allow dogs may transition easily into your home, regardless of what other types of dogs you have owned in the past. A 90-pound (41-kg) Rottweiler who was given up due to growling and other threatening behaviors, on the other hand, will need considerable training by someone with specific experience dealing with aggression problems.

If you live with other people, you also must consider if they are ready for dog adoption. The entire household should be involved in the decision-making process. Having a plan in place before you adopt is ideal. Who will share the responsibility of caring for the dog? Who will help to train him? If there are children in the household, are they old enough to understand and demonstrate the proper way to treat a pet? If kids will be helping to care for the dog, who will be following up to make sure important tasks aren't forgotten?

No one, not even a person who lives alone, should enter dog ownership without a proper support system. Rescue volunteers and trainers can be invaluable resources for information regarding pet care, but occasionally you will need some help carrying out certain tasks as well. Ask your friends and family if they would be willing to help you when necessary. You will need someone to feed your dog and take him outside when you have to work late, for instance, or to care for him overnight when you travel. If your friends aren't as fond of dogs as you are or if you have just moved to a new area and don't know many people yet, you will need to find a reputable dog daycare or pet sitter instead.

Before bringing an adopted dog into your life, make sure that you are willing to invest the time and money necessary to fulfill all his needs—both physical and emotional.

If you choose to adopt, your most important job will be finding the right dog for you. You may not be able to fulfill your lifelong dream of rescuing a Saint Bernard—not just yet anyway—but you may find that a Golden Retriever possesses many of the qualities that drew you to Saints in the first place. You may even discover that a dog needn't have a pedigree at all to capture your heart. Once you find the dog who is right for you, you can then take the next step in your journey to changing both his life and yours through the rewarding process of adoption.

C h a p t e r

WHERE
to Adopt a Dog

eciding where to start the search for your adopted dog can seem more than a little overwhelming at first. With so many dogs in need of new homes, where is the best place to find one that will match your lifestyle? Should you adopt from your local animal shelter or from a breed rescue? How do you find a rescue group dedicated to the breed you like best? What can the volunteers tell you about the dog you are considering adopting?

ANIMAL SHELTERS AND HUMANE SOCIETIES

Today, most unwanted dogs are brought to animal shelters. These establishments, while far from luxurious, provide homeless animals with food, refuge, and the chance for new homes and families. Shelters evolved from what were once called "dog pounds." These facilities, which consisted of little more than cages for stray animals, had one main goal: containing the animals. During the 19th century, free-roaming dogs posed significant problems to people. In rural areas, they frequently helped themselves to the farmers' crops, and many attacked livestock. In urban areas, they damaged property and sometimes acted aggressively toward people they encountered.

At that time, dogs were primarily viewed as property. Therefore, the people who ran dog pounds did not concern themselves with treating the animals humanely. As people began to see dogs as living beings, however, they began to recognize problems with the way that stray animals were being handled. In 1840, the first humane society, the Royal Society for the Prevention of Cruelty to Animals (RSPCA), was founded in Great Britain. In 1866, an American philanthropist named Henry Burgh proposed a similar idea to the New York state legislature, and the American Society for the Prevention of Cruelty to Animals (ASPCA) was born. Along with it came the first anti-cruelty laws in the United States.

Common Reasons Dogs Are Surrendered to Shelters and Breed Rescue Groups

Some people assume that a dog must have done something wrong to be surrendered to a shelter or rescue group. In actuality, though, most dogs are in need of new homes due to no fault of their own. Here are just a few of the reasons they are surrendered:

- owner moved to an apartment that didn' t allow dogs
- owner moved to an assisted living facility
- owner passed away
- owners got divorced
- owner had allergies
- owner' s financial situation changed
- owners had a new baby
- dog was an unwanted gift
- dog turned out to be more than owner could handle (too large, too active, etc.)
- dog was found as a stray
- dog was seized by authorities (from either abusive owners or breeders)

In the last century, numerous humane societies, both national and local, have been established around the United States. Many operate their own animal shelters, but the largest ones focus their energies on promoting education and developing legislation for the proper treatment of animals. Larger organizations also help create the guidelines that other smaller animal shelters across the country follow.

Public animal shelters still provide refuge for impounded dogs (each county within a state usually has its own shelter), but most also accept dogs from individual owners who wish to surrender their animals. These government-run shelters rely on a number of resources for income, including dog licensing fees, fines for violations of dog laws, and grants. Private shelters receive no financial assistance from the government. Because of this, they are free to choose which animals they accept, but many make agreements with local animal control departments to care for stray animals picked up by the animal warden.

Both public and private shelters usually require owners to contribute an adoption fee when they adopt a dog. The amount varies from shelter to shelter, but invariably it is less than the cost of buying a dog from a pet store or breeder. Some shelters charge a higher fee for puppies and popular breeds that they know will find new owners more easily. This helps the shelter care for dogs who stay at the shelter longer. Remember, you can always give more than the standard amount. If you adopt a dog from a shelter and you can afford to donate more than the requested fee, please do so. Every little bit of revenue makes a difference. An additional donation of just a few dollars can buy 10 pounds (4.5 kg) of dry dog food for the animals still awaiting their own adoptive owners. If there's one thing almost every shelter needs just as much as people to adopt their animals, it is money. Some even sell pet care items such as collars and leashes as a means of raising additional funds for their facilities.

Shelters are always in need of extra sets of hands, too. The majority of people who volunteer want to work directly with the animals, and certainly this is a big part of what needs to be done. All the dogs at a shelter need to be fed and walked regularly, and they also benefit greatly from interaction with volunteers. But other jobs must be done to keep a shelter running. Cages must be cleaned, bedding and towels must be laundered, and clerical work must be kept up to date. If you would be interested in performing any of these tasks for your local shelter, let them know. Most facilities hold regular orientations for new volunteers, and they welcome any help they can get. This will also give you a chance to get to know the animals

Animal shelters and humane societies provide homeless animals with food, refuge, and the chance for new homes and families.

Although shelters usually charge an adoption fee, it is invariably much less than the cost of buying a dog from a pet store or breeder.

and perhaps to find one particular individual who captures your heart and possibly finds a place in your home.

Because the populations at shelters grow so rapidly, they are forced to make the heart-wrenching decision of which animals are the most likely to get adopted and which ones probably won't. Although as many as 60 to 75 percent of dogs surrendered by owners to shelters are adopted, another 25 to 40 percent are not. The latter group is typically given a certain amount of time before they are placed on the shelters' euthanasia lists. Most are aggressive dogs and those with severe health problems, but this canine death row also frequently includes older pets and ones who simply haven't caught the eyes of adoptive owners. Some states have laws that require all dogs entering a shelter to be held for a minimum number of days or weeks before being euthanized. If they are adopted within this time period, their new families save them from being put to sleep.

You may have heard of no-kill shelters. These organizations have become quite popular in recent years because of their universal policy of never euthanizing a single animal they admit. While this may be an admirable goal, one must realize that such shelters have to be extremely selective about which animals they accept. A no-kill facility must turn away all dogs who are unlikely to be adopted in a reasonable amount of time. If they didn't do this, their populations of unadoptable animals would climb progressively until the shelters ran out of both space and money. Most of the dogs these shelters reject are then brought to conventional shelters, where they are euthanized nonetheless if they are not adopted within a certain time period.

Why Adopt From a Shelter?

Animal shelters are considered to be the grassroots organizations working hardest to eliminate the growing unwanted pet population problem. Adopting a dog from a shelter is an excellent means of "thinking globally but acting locally." When you adopt a dog in your area, you are helping your own community. You also provide a wonderful example to other people who may be considering adoption.

Adopting from a shelter is ideal for anyone who wants a dog but isn't concerned about having a particular breed. This doesn't mean that owners cannot find the specific type of dog they are looking for at shelters. For example, you may tell the counselor with whom you meet that you would like a friendly, medium-sized dog with short hair. Chances are good that you

Gimmie a Clean Shelter

Use the same level of scrutiny in evaluating a shelter as you would in selecting a breeding kennel. While shelters don't have to be filled with fancy amenities, they should be clean. A faint smell of bleach is usually a good sign. Because so many dogs are housed together in shelters, diseases can spread quickly if reasonable precautions aren't taken.

Ideally, cages should include solid partitions between animals. Nose-to-nose contact through chain-link fences can spread a number of dangerous diseases, including distemper and parvovirus. Even if a dog is vaccinated upon arriving at a shelter, the protection is not immediate. Many vaccines require additional booster shots before they are considered fully effective. Feces should be removed as soon as a dog eliminates, and each cage should be cleaned regularly to prevent the spread of worms and other feces-spread diseases. A clean environment is a good indication that the staff treats the animals properly in other ways as well.

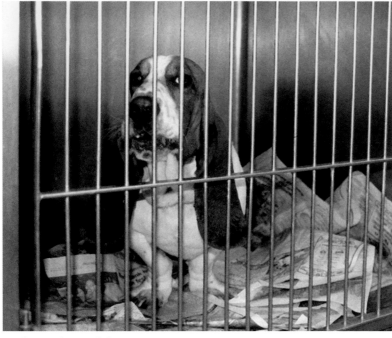

Adopting from a shelter is ideal for anyone who wants a dog but isn't concerned about having a particular breed.

will find a dog to fit this description. He may even end up being a purebred.

Shelters can usually tell you a lot more about a particular dog than how he looks. Highly trained volunteers assess both the health and temperament of each animal admitted to the facility. When an animal is relinquished, shelter workers also do their best to collect as much information about a dog's history as possible. Most shelters continue to observe the animal before clearing him for adoption to help ensure that all the information gathered matches up. The shelter's biggest goal is to find a permanent, loving home for each of its animals. The best way to accomplish this is to help prospective owners identify the best dogs for them.

Most shelters provide adoption counseling as well as follow-up services such as training classes for interested owners. A shelter can also refer new owners to reputable veterinarians, groomers, and other professionals who provide animal-related services in their area. When you adopt a dog from a shelter, he should be vaccinated, dewormed, and neutered by the time you take him home. Some shelters also microchip each pet prior to placement. While your adoption fee certainly helps pay for all this, it far from covers the total costs that a shelter incurs. Adoptive owners pay far less for these veterinary services than people who purchase dogs from breeders or pet shops.

Anyone who adopts a dog helps save a life, but this is especially true of those who choose to adopt from shelters. While breed rescues also work to place homeless dogs, these animals are far more likely to find new owners than are shelter dogs. If you adopt a dog from a shelter, you could literally be saving his life.

The Drawbacks of Shelter Adoption

Some states have privacy laws that prevent shelters from sharing information about a dog's history with his new owner. The purpose of these laws is to protect those who surrender their animals, effectively encouraging people who no longer want their dogs to give them up instead of neglecting or abusing them or simply setting them free. Unfortunately, this leaves both shelters and new owners in a difficult position. Without reliable information, both volunteers and the people interested in adopting must rely on observation and speculation when determining an individual dog's history and temperament.

At times, people who relinquish animals to shelters lie about the particulars of their situations. Some may worry that the shelter won't take the dog if they admit that he is ill. Others may fear that the dog will be euthanized if they tell the shelter that he bites. The worst scenarios involve mistreatment, something no owner ever admits to voluntarily. No matter what their reasons, most people who surrender pets hold back at least

Without reliable information, shelter volunteers and the people interested in adopting must rely on observation and speculation when determining an individual dog's history and temperament.

Brought to You by Dog Lovers Everywhere

Some shelters offer dog lovers a unique way of helping animals in need. By sponsoring a shelter dog, you give a homeless animal more time to find an adoptive family. Many shelters offer sponsorships for a small monthly fee. Some even allow donors to visit and play with their sponsored pets. Sponsorship is a wonderful thing for anyone who wants to make a difference, but it is an especially smart alternative for people who aren't ready to adopt pets of their own.

some information; others try to outright mislead the shelter volunteers. Most shelter workers have become remarkably capable of sensing when a person leaving a pet is being less than upfront with them, but even the best intake workers can be fooled sometimes.

When it comes to strays, shelters have little means of knowing what happened to the animals before their arrival. Being on the street for a long period of time also changes a dog. A stray could have been born on the street, or he might have had a wonderful home and an amiable temperament at some point in his past. Once he ran away from home and had to fend for himself on the streets, however, a number of unfortunate events could have ensued. These experiences further shape the dog's temperament and even affect his ultimate trainability.

Many female strays come to shelters with a litter of pups on the way. In these situations, it is impossible to predict what the offspring will look like or what their temperaments will be. If both parents are small dogs, the pups will probably also be diminutive in size. If the unknown father was a bigger dog, however, the pups may grow to be much larger than their mother. A dog's temperament is affected far more by his environment than his genetics, but certain qualities such as prey drive or how active a dog is are determined primarily by the breeds in his lineage.

While most shelters maintain waiting lists for people looking for certain breeds, they cannot guarantee that a particular breed will ever become available. Frequently, by the time a shelter calls the person who wanted a Pembroke Welsh Corgi, that person has already found one elsewhere. If you want to adopt a specific breed, your best bet is a breed rescue.

BREED RESCUE ORGANIZATIONS

Toward the end of the 20th century, breed rescue organizations were founded as another means of matching potential owners with dogs in need of new homes. Rescues help to lessen the number of dogs animal shelters must handle each day. Unlike shelters, though, each breed rescue group focuses its attention on a single dog breed. Both national and local breed rescue groups exist for nearly every dog breed. Most local groups work under the rules and guidelines set forth by the breed's national rescue organization.

Rescue volunteers are often breeders and breed club members who use their knowledge and experience with their chosen breed to find each dog his best possible home. Some rescue groups ask owners who intend to relinquish their dogs to first speak with one of the rescue's breed experts. By providing direction and encouragement to these owners, they can prevent some dogs from being given up at all.

Certain breed rescues focus their attention on a group of related breeds, such as spaniels or terriers, for example. Most of these multi-breed rescues utilize the expertise of a variety of volunteers. Some of them may have experience with only a single type of dog; others may breed or own two or more of the breeds. One of the biggest advantages of adopting through a breed rescue is the amount of experience the volunteers bring to the job. If one person can't answer your questions, someone else surely can.

Unlike shelters, breed rescue groups focus their attention on a single dog breed. They may also specialize in placing dogs of specific breed mixes, like this handsome Bouvier des Flandres mix.

Not all rescue volunteers are experts, though. Many are owners just like you. Volunteering is actually a smart way of learning all you can about a particular breed before you decide that it's the right one for you. Even if you end up deciding that a particular breed doesn't match your lifestyle, the time you spend helping the dogs find new homes is never wasted. On the contrary, it may be one of the most rewarding tasks you ever undertake.

Breed rescues may also specialize in placing dogs of specific breed mixes. Cockapoos, Goldendoodles, and Puggles, just to name a few, all have their own rescue organizations in a variety of

areas. If you are looking for a particular breed mix, one of these organizations is your best bet.

In some cases, a rescue is a one-person show, a single volunteer placing just one or two dogs at a time. Although larger rescue organizations often place up to 300 dogs a year, a single-person operation may place only a dozen or fewer. It is difficult to know exactly how many dogs are saved through rescue because there is no governing body to manage the process or keep a tally, yet every dog placed is a dog saved.

Like animal shelters, breed rescue organizations require owners to pay an adoption fee. The amount can vary from one group to another; it can even be different for certain dogs, depending on their individual circumstances. Like shelters, rescue groups will gladly accept donations above their requested amount. Some even hold regular fundraisers. The more money and other resources rescue groups have, the more dogs they can help place. These events are commonly held at pet supply stores, and they offer the public a chance to contribute, as well as to meet, some of the dogs in need of homes.

To find the nearest rescue group for the breed of your choice, contact your local humane society. Most of these organizations keep lists of rescues in their respective geographic regions. Your veterinarian also may be able to direct you to someone in your area who does this important work. Often, the smaller groups are less well known, but they can be every bit as helpful in matching you with a great dog. Some rescue groups will also advertise their available dogs in the classified sections of local newspapers.

The Benefits of Finding a Dog Through a Breed Rescue

In addition to providing adoptive owners with a fast track to specific breeds, rescue groups offer various other advantages as well. Perhaps the most significant of these is a well-documented history of each dog. While rare exceptions exist, breed rescues usually obtain a great deal of information about the dogs they place because they speak at length with each dog's previous owner. Moreover, they can share this

In addition to providing adoptive owners with a fast track to specific breeds, breed rescues usually obtain a great deal of information about the dogs they place because they frequently stay in touch with the owners of dogs they home.

information with potential adoptive owners because they are not bound by the same privacy laws as shelters.

In addition to more serious information, such as whether the dog has any allergies or behavior issues, rescue groups also can provide new owners with helpful details such as the type of food the dog eats and what kinds of toys are his favorites. Ask as many questions as possible about the dog you are considering. The volunteers may or may not know the answers, but if they do, they will surely share them with you. Gathering as much information as possible about your new pet can help make his transition into your home and family a smooth one.

A breed rescue spends a great deal of time and effort evaluating its dogs before placing them with new owners. Rescue workers also screen potential adoptive owners and their families, so the best possible match can be made for every dog. If a dog has special needs, the volunteers make sure that he is placed with an owner who is both willing and able to provide him with appropriate care. At times, new owners may find this process to be a bit intimidating, but rest assured that the volunteers overseeing placement always have the best interest of the dogs in mind.

Because each one only deals with a single breed, rescue groups tend to be extremely knowledgeable about the breeds they place. If you are unsure whether an Australian Shepherd is the right adoptee for you, rescue volunteers are your best resources for gathering the information you need to make your decision. Unlike shelter workers, most of these people actually live with the breed you are considering. They know both the ups and downs of owning this kind of dog, and they can share their personal stories with you.

When a dog is surrendered to a rescue group, a volunteer within that rescue community provides the animal with a temporary home or more lengthy foster care. Although some shelter volunteers also provide foster care, it is the norm rather than the exception for breed rescues. Because dogs in breed rescues are afforded this special one-on-one time, volunteers can give potential owners a great deal of insight into what it will be like to live with each dog. For example, a certain dog may have shown his foster family that he needs some remedial housetraining or that he would do best in a home without cats.

The Drawbacks of Breed Rescue Adoption

Sadly, some people get involved in dog rescue to help themselves more than the dogs they place. A rescue need not be large or well known to be trustworthy, but it should always be a nonprofit organization. Beware of rescues that demand extraordinarily high fees for the dogs they place. Also, be suspicious if a rescue is willing to give you a dog without interviewing you personally. A rescue group such as this

Ending the Overpopulation Problem

Most animal shelters and breed rescue organizations require that every dog be spayed or neutered prior to being placed with a new owner. It is often an unplanned pregnancy that lands a litter of pups in rescue shelters. The people who work to place such animals want to make sure that these puppies don't contribute to the overpopulation problem as adults. As much as you think it won't happen to your dog, accidents do happen. As unbelievable as it may seem, a female dog and her offspring can produce as many as 67,000 puppies in just 6 years. The only way to prevent unwanted canine pregnancies with 100 percent certainty is to have every pet spayed or neutered.

The biggest drawback to adopting from a breed rescue is that you may have to travel a long way to meet with a group that deals with your breed of choice.

definitely does not have the best interest of the animals in mind. Some will even place dogs with known behavior problems without disclosing this information to the prospective owner. Fortunately, reputable rescue organizations do care about the dogs they adopt out, but owners must always be vigilant nonetheless.

At times, prospective owners prefer to deal with animal shelters because of the high expectations that breed rescue organizations have for their animals' care. Some feel intimidated by having to pass screenings that may include an extensive interview and a home visit before being allowed to adopt a dog. If you can relate to this, try to bear in mind that rescue volunteers want things to work out for both you and the dog you wish to adopt. They aren't looking for trivial reasons to deny ownership; they just want to make sure that you will provide the dog with a safe, happy, and permanent home.

The biggest stumbling block to adopting a dog through a breed rescue is actually geography. Some adoptive owners find that they must travel a long way to meet with a group that deals with their breed of choice. Breed rescues tend to cover specific

Online Search and Rescue

Before the Internet emerged, animal shelters relied primarily on foot traffic to find adoptive owners for their animals. Now, however, shelters and breed rescues alike can post online photos and detailed descriptions of the pets they have available for adoption. You can look for a particular type of dog or peruse the list of current residents at your local shelter right from the comfort of your own home.

The web has been especially helpful for breed rescues because so many have no actual place of business but instead work out of the homes of various volunteers. Anyone interested in learning more about a particular rescue can do so online anytime, anywhere. Most shelters and rescues also provide information about their adoption processes and fees on their websites.

The following are some of the wonderful online resources available for locating dogs in need of new homes across the United States. You can narrow your search to your own area or travel as far as you'd like in order to find the right dog for you:

- ASPCA: www.aspca.org/adoption/shelters
- Humane America Animal Foundation's adoption agency: www.1-800-save-a-pet.com
- AKC's National Breed Club Rescue Network: www.akc.org/breeds/rescue.cfm
- Big Paws Rescue (specializing in giant dog breeds): www.bigpawsrescue.tripod.com
- Pet Shelter Network: www.petshelternetwork.org
- Petfinder.com: www.petfinder.com
- Senior Canine Rescue Society: www.seniordogrescue.org

It is important to remember, though, that the Internet is just a starting point. Always meet with the shelter or rescue volunteers in person before committing to adopting an animal. And never agree to adopt a dog you haven't met face to face.

If you prefer to search for a pet in person, you can find listings for animal shelters, humane societies, and breed rescue groups in your area by checking your local yellow pages. Every year, the *AKC Gazette* publishes a list of breed rescue organizations for all national breed clubs in its November issue. (You can also find information about rescues at the AKC website, www.akc.org.) You may even be able to find a dog in need of adoption by visiting your local pet supply store. Some retailers act as adoption liaisons by donating space in their stores to local animal shelters. By 2007, more than 3 million pets throughout the United States and Canada were adopted through these adoption day events.

territories. For example, Yankee Golden Retriever Rescue serves all six New England states. Based in Massachusetts, this rescue may be several hours away from a potential adoptive owner. While long drives can be frustrating, most new owners agree that finding the dog of their dreams was well worth the added effort.

IS THERE AN END IN SIGHT?

Many concerned individuals wonder if there will ever come a time when a need for animal shelters and breed rescue organizations no longer exists. It is easy to get discouraged when contemplating the number of animals who enter shelters each day. Although dog ownership in the United States has increased in recent years, the number of dogs surrendered to shelters and rescue organizations has also risen. To tirelessly dedicated volunteers, the rescue process may at times feel like taking a few steps forward and nearly as many steps backward.

Animal rights organizations exist in large part to put an end to the suffering—and ultimate homelessness—of dogs everywhere. Toward this worthy goal, however, some lobby for governments to pass anti-breeding laws that would prohibit both puppy mills and responsible hobby breeders alike from breeding dogs. The mere proposal of such indiscriminate legislation enormously complicates this profoundly difficult problem.

While none of us can predict what the future holds, one thing is certain: Dogs in animal shelters and breed rescue groups throughout the country need new homes right now. The only chance we have for solving this problem is finding each dog a loving home, one owner at a time.

What About "Free to Good Home" Ads?

Advertisements in local newspapers or flyers pinned to pet supply store bulletin boards sometimes offer dogs as "free to good home." You may wonder if this is a good way to go about adopting a pet. As a prospective adoptive owner, you might find an excellent dog this way—and may even save him from ever entering an animal shelter. Owners who offer their pets for free are often well intended. They are more interested in finding good homes for their pets than being paid back for their financial investment in them.

If you go this route, however, you should understand that you have no recourse if something goes wrong. If the owner misrepresents the situation—for example, if you find out after you take the dog that he is a biter—the original owner is under no obligation to take him back. You are then faced with the horrible decision of whether you should keep or surrender him.

3

FINDING
the Right Dog for You

I f there's one thing a successful adoption hinges upon, it is finding the dog who is right for you and your family. Most people can make ideal adoptive owners if paired with the right dogs, but an inappropriate choice can be disastrous for all involved. If you have made the decision that you want to get a dog through adoption, the next step is carefully selecting the animal whose needs best match your experience, abilities, and even your own personality.

Nearly all dogs in need of new homes come with a certain amount of baggage. For some, this is as simple as a pesky habit of begging at the dinner table; for others it may be more serious, such as a deeply ingrained fear of people. A dog who whines while his owners eat can be redirected with a scrumptious chew toy at meal time. If offering a toy doesn't do the trick, a handful of other basic strategies can help eliminate this common canine behavior problem. A dog who has been abused, however, may need weeks (or even months) of intense work before any behavior issues he has can be corrected.

Adoptive owners must be patient and kind, but these venerable qualities alone are not enough. Certain breeds and breed mixes have very specific behavior traits. Some are much more stubborn than others. Age also plays a part in how a dog responds to a new owner and environment. Adoptive owners must be able to engage their dogs and hold their attention during training sessions and be willing to adapt their strategies to match the needs of a specific animal. For example, some dogs enjoy being outdoors and are better able to focus in this environment. Other dogs are highly motivated by food; these animals will learn most quickly when given both praise and edible rewards for their progress.

If a good rapport is established between an owner and a dog, the chances for success multiply tenfold.

ADOPTING A PUPPY

Adopting a puppy is in many ways the best of both worlds. You are rescuing a dog

When adopting a dog, carefully select an animal whose needs best match your experience, abilities, and even your own personality.

in need of a home and getting him while most of his life still lies ahead of him. Most puppies also possess an undeniable cuteness factor. Just because a dog is young, however, doesn't mean that he hasn't developed some behaviors that need correcting. Adopting a puppy is not the same thing as buying a puppy from a breeder.

Puppy Love

One of the biggest benefits to adopting a puppy is that his new owners can help shape his personality. The younger a dog is when you adopt him, the more influence you will have on his behavior and temperament as an adult. Much depends on the puppy's earliest experiences, however. Proper socialization between the ages of three weeks and three months usually translates into a friendly, well-adjusted dog. Conversely, a lack of exposure to people during this time period can leave a dog timid or aloof. Knowing a puppy's history (however short) is therefore a major advantage in training him.

It's commonly thought that puppies are easier to train than adult dogs. While this assertion depends on the individual animal, most puppies do delight in being praised. Combine this enthusiasm with a breed or mix that's known for a strong desire to please his owner and you will likely end up with a highly trainable animal.

Puppies tend to be much more approachable than adult dogs. This can make ongoing socialization an easier task for puppy owners. Even a breed that looks more intimidating, such as a Rottweiler or German Shepherd, can prompt complete strangers to approach you at the park and implore, "May I pet your puppy?"

Pint-Sized Problems

As much fun as puppies can be, adopting a younger dog can be a lot of work. Even if a puppy is already on his way to being housetrained when you adopt him, it will still be a while before he is reliable in this regard. A dog is rarely fully housetrained until he is at least several months old. Another exasperating issue puppy owners must deal with is teething. Dogs don't outgrow their need to chew, but younger dogs must be taught which items are acceptable chew toys. It is a rare dog who never mistakes one of his owner's shoes for a chew toy at least a few times during puppyhood.

If you have younger children, an adult dog may be a much better choice for your family. Many of the adult dogs surrendered to shelters have already lived with children and know what to expect from them. An adult dog's size alone makes him more fit for living with older children. Toddlers who are just learning to walk themselves can injure (or even kill) a puppy by falling on him. Kids too can be hurt if a puppy feels his safety is threatened. While most young children are fascinated by puppies, the puppies may be easily frightened by these loud, rambunctious little people. Younger dogs often react poorly to having their ears or tails pulled. Puppies typically have mighty sharp teeth, and they lack the restraint that comes with thorough training and maturity.

During his first few weeks as part of your household, a very young puppy may cry at night. As someone who has been in this situation, I liken the experience to having a human infant

As much fun as puppies can be, adopting a younger dog can be a lot of work.

in the house. Even the most patient person in the world can have a hard time dealing with persistent noise and sleep loss. Although weaned puppies do not need to eat in the middle of the night as human babies do, they may need to be taken to their potty spot for elimination. Sometimes puppies cry simply because they are in an unfamiliar environment. This usually passes once the dog gets a little older and more accustomed to living in your home, but in the meantime it can be very stressful for anyone within earshot.

Perhaps the biggest reason not to adopt a puppy if you're not sure you can offer him a permanent home is that he will likely be adopted by someone else if you don't take him. This can't always be said for adult dogs. Remember, full-grown yet still young dogs are available through both shelters and rescue groups.

ADOPTING AN ADULT DOG

On average, a dog enters adulthood around the time that he reaches two years of age; smaller dogs mature a bit earlier, larger ones a bit later. Many adoptive owners prefer adult dogs, and the reasons can be as varied as the individuals and the dogs they save. While few animal lovers can resist smiling when they see a puppy, some fanciers like the look of a fully grown dog better than that of a pup. Larger breeds, specifically, look amazingly different once they have reached their full size. Even more important than physical appearance, however, is the adult dog's personality, which is much more clearly defined at maturity.

The Benefits of Choosing a Mature Pet

Most dogs in need of adoption require some training. Believe it or not, adult dogs are often easier to train than young puppies. They usually have longer attention spans than their younger counterparts. Whereas a puppy can be distracted easily by everyday occurrences, such as the mail carrier's arrival or a leaf blowing through the backyard, an adult dog doesn't need to chase either one to know what they are. He has probably, as they say, "been there and done that." He is ready for something a bit more stimulating.

Adult dogs at shelters and rescues are not only ready to be trained, but many also may be ready to join their new owners in a number of fun activities. If you enjoy jogging, adopting a puppy means waiting a while before he is physically fit to join you. Adopting an active adult dog, however, can mean having an instant running companion. A

Dogs Are Trainable at Any Age

You may assume that adopting an older dog means that his training days are behind him. When it comes to tasks such as housetraining, this is generally the case. Most adoptive owners even consider this to be a perk to owning a senior pet. It doesn't mean, however, that your mature dog is too old to learn new things. Like people, dogs benefit from learning at any age. The best way to keep your older dog's mind sharp is by giving him opportunities to use it every day. Buy him puzzle toys that dispense yummy treats when rolled the right way, or teach him a new command. Maybe your older dog walks nicely on his leash, but does he know how to heel? Did he ever learn to shake hands? If not, it's never too late. Older pets have better attention spans than young ones, making them ideal students. Perhaps most importantly, they enjoy pleasing their owners and being praised for a job well done just as much as their younger counterparts.

growing canine body is extremely more susceptible to injury and overexertion than an adult's. Because of this, certain organized activities for dogs—agility, for instance—include minimum ages for involvement.

If your idea of a good time is renting a movie and hanging out on the sofa, an adult dog may be a good match for you, too. Just be sure to select one with a lower need for exercise. Adult dogs in general are past their most energetic phase. They still need regular exercise and playtime, of course, but playing ball with them doesn't equate to spring training with the Red Sox. The volunteers at a shelter or rescue group also can help you identify the best couch potato for you.

Senior adult dogs make amazing pets for the right people. If you are older yourself, you may enjoy the company of a dog who walks a little more slowly and sleeps a little bit longer. You may also prefer an older dog if you have a hectic schedule and aren't home enough to manage tasks such as housetraining. The majority of older dogs have already been housetrained, and while daily interaction is a must, these more mature canines don't require the constant supervision that puppies do.

Adult dogs at shelters and rescues are not only ready to be trained, but many also may be ready to join their new owners in a number of fun activities.

Although a surprising number of purebred dogs are available for adoption at animal shelters, finding a particular breed may be difficult.

Grown-Up Issues

Some owners prefer adopting the youngest dogs possible because they want to put as much time as they can between bringing their dogs home and having to say goodbye to them. The most obvious disadvantage to adopting an older pet is indeed that you may have less time with him than with a younger adoptee. One should put this assumption into perspective, though. Due to the advancement of veterinary medicine and the more we continue to learn about healthy canine lifestyles, dogs are living longer than ever before. Quality of life for all senior pets, and especially for those living with chronic conditions, has also has improved greatly over the last couple of decades. There is no guarantee that an adult dog will live a certain number of years, but there is no guarantee that a puppy will either. If you find an adult dog with all the qualities you are looking for in a canine companion, don't concentrate on the years that lie behind him. Focus on today and all the tomorrows that lie ahead of the two of you.

ADOPTING A PUREBRED DOG

If you have your heart set on adopting a purebred dog, you may find him at your local shelter, but you will probably have better luck contacting a breed rescue group. Although a

The Best Breeds for Children

If you have children, your first consideration in selecting a dog is determining how well a particular breed gets along with kids. Just as certain types of dogs are poor choices for families with young children, others are known for their child-friendly dispositions. Unfortunately, many dogs in need of new homes have been mistreated—some by kids, which can drastically affect an individual dog's reactions toward younger people. Be sure to tell the volunteers at your local shelter or breed rescue that you have children so that they can direct you toward the dogs in their care who are best suited to your personal circumstances. The following is a list of some of the best breeds and breed mixes for families with kids:

- Beagles and Hound Mixes
- Bichons Frises
- Bulldogs
- Golden Retrievers, Labrador Retrievers, and Retriever Mixes
- Greyhounds
- Newfoundlands
- Poodles and Poodle Mixes
- Pugs
- Saint Bernards

Remember, dogs and kids must always be supervised when together. The best behaved child can inadvertently hurt a dog by just trying to play with him, and the best tempered dog can run out of patience when treated inappropriately.

surprising number of purebred dogs are available for adoption at animal shelters, finding a particular breed can be difficult, especially if you want a less common one. Not too many Dandie Dinmont Terriers, for example, can be found at shelters.

The word "purebred" is a bit of a contradiction. Although breeders and other fanciers have been working to preserve the lineage of different dog breeds for hundreds of years, there isn't a single dog whose lineage is truly "pure." Every breed, at one point or another, has been crossed with another breed. Saint Bernards, for example, were outcrossed with Newfoundlands in the 1800s. The former breed's population declined sharply when numerous Saints perished doing their trademark rescue work. The introduction of Newfoundlands into the bloodlines saved the Saint Bernard breed from extinction. Similar outcrosses have been made to save various breeds from dying out, as well as for aesthetic reasons, such as coat color and texture. The result of this practice is a diverse group of breeds that are more closely related than many pet owners realize.

Pure Joy

Purebred dogs can make wonderful pets for the right people. Each breed possesses its own unique set of qualities that make it ideal for a specific type of owner. If you want a swimming companion, the Portuguese Water Dog may be a fitting choice. If you are an avid hunter, check out the German Short-Haired Pointer. Prefer a more portable breed that you can take with you nearly everywhere? Consider a Yorkshire Terrier. Currently, more than 150 breeds are officially recognized by the American Kennel Club (AKC). You are sure to find at least one that matches your lifestyle.

Some breeds are known for being smart and highly trainable. Poodles, for example, are often touted as being especially bright dogs. Having owned one as a child, I can attest to this personally. Other breeds are known for their loyalty; Akitas frequently top this list. Many small breeds, like Havanese, have been bred for centuries to be superlative lap dogs.

Owning a purebred dog can be a lot of fun. Joining a breed club, for instance, is a great way to meet new people who share your interest in your favorite dog breed. Through my work and personal life, I have met countless people who share my love for Cocker Spaniels. Many of them have become dear friends.

Purebred dogs can make wonderful pets for the right people. Each breed possesses its own unique set of qualities that make it ideal for a specific type of owner.

Not So Fast!

It is commonly thought that Greyhounds need to live with owners who are as athletic as they are, but this isn't the case at all! Certainly every dog needs exercise — and this breed does love to run — but most retired racing dogs are ready to live their lives at a more leisurely pace. This doesn't mean that only older Greyhounds are available for adoption. Most are retired around the age of four and have long lifetimes ahead of them; the lifespan of these dogs is often 14 years or more. Greyhound owners do need to be careful to keep their pets leashed outdoors, however, because sighthounds will run after squirrels and other small animals if the opportunity arises. Still, these graceful and energetic dogs are sprinters, not marathon runners, so even a moderately active person can usually keep up with them.

Some people have owned particular breeds all their lives. I have friends who will adopt nothing other than Golden Retrievers. Others swear by Labradors. If you have found a dog breed that works for you, sticking with it can be a great way to help ensure that the home you share with your adopted dog will be a happy one.

Each dog is an individual, of course. Oftentimes owners are amazed by just how different two dogs of the same breed can be, but dogs of the same breed do share many qualities. This leaves room for far fewer surprises.

That being said, some individuals prefer to own purebreds but also are open to offering a new home to dogs of all types. One friend of mine has adopted three different dogs in the 25 years I have known him. As a person who prefers larger breeds, two of these dogs have been purebreds—a Siberian Husky and a Chow Chow. The third, which he adopted just recently, is a Collie-Shepherd mix, although he looks almost entirely like a German Shepherd. Each of my friend's dogs has been unique, but all have made wonderful companion pets for him regardless of breed.

NO BREED IS PERFECT

Some people think that purebred dogs are better than mixed-breed dogs. Even as a proud owner of purebreds, I strongly disagree with this stance. Mixed breeds can make equally wonderful pets. One may even argue that mixes offer some clear advantages over dogs with conformation champions in their lineage.

Every dog breed, no matter how rare or popular, is prone to certain health problems. For instance, English Springer Spaniels are predisposed to eye problems. One affliction in particular, called progressive retinal atrophy (PRA), causes irreversible blindness. Labrador Retrievers frequently suffer from hip problems. Because they have such tiny mouths, and therefore crowded teeth, Chihuahuas and other toy breeds are especially susceptible to tooth decay. But rather than focusing just on shortcomings, you must consider a dog's overall qualities when choosing a canine companion that is best suited to your own personality and lifestyle.

If you adopt a particular breed because of its fancy

appearance, be prepared to spend a lot of time grooming. Longhaired dogs, like the Lhasa Apso and the Briard, need to be brushed every day to prevent nasty snarls from forming in their coats. Certain shorthaired breeds, like the Bulldog and the Chinese Shar-Pei, need frequent grooming because their wrinkles must be cleaned daily to prevent skin infections. Even if you manage to keep your adopted purebred free of tangles or every skin fold squeaky clean, there's another consideration to bear in mind: You won't be able to show your adopted purebred because nearly all shelters and rescues require mandatory sterilization of the pets they place. Spayed and neutered dogs are not eligible to compete in conformation events, which were formed over a century ago as a means of evaluating breeding stock.

MIXED BREEDS

There are two different types of mixed-breed dogs. So-called "designer breeds" have been created by crossing various pairs of different purebred dogs. Dozens of designer dog breeds have been created in the last decade or two, but some have been around for much longer than this. Two of the most popular designer dogs are the Cockapoo, a hybrid of the American Cocker Spaniel and the Poodle, and the Labradoodle, a hybrid of the Labrador Retriever and the Poodle. Poodles are among the most common dogs used in this increasingly popular

Love Can Be Blind, Deaf, or Diabetic

Many dogs in need of new homes have disabilities or chronic conditions. Some have lost their eyesight, hearing, or even a limb. Others might suffer from diabetes or epilepsy. Some people are intimated by the idea of assuming the care of such dogs, but owning a special-needs pet is usually much easier than they fear. Most conditions bother the owners far more than they limit the dogs themselves, and many require only minimal intervention on behalf of caregivers. A good friend of mine has a blind dog who can catch a scented tennis ball. I myself own an epileptic dog. While I certainly don't enjoy watching my dog experience a seizure, these episodes are thankfully both short and infrequent. At any other time, one would never guess that Molly has a chronic condition at all. She runs and plays just like any other animal. Many health problems, from diabetes to thyroid issues, can be managed easily with medications. Owning a dog with this kind of problem often means spending a bit more time and money, but these are extraordinarily worthwhile investments. Caring for a dog with a chronic condition has taught me a lot about compassion, acceptance, and perseverance. Special-needs dogs have a lot to give—in love and life lessons.

practice because of their intelligence and loving natures. The Puggle, a cross of the Pug and the Beagle, is another very popular mixed breed.

More common than designer dog breeds is the mutt. Mutts can have any number of breeds in their lineage. Unlike purebred and designer mixes, however, most mutts are the product of chance encounters between their parents. Very few people breed mutts intentionally, but by failing to spay or neuter their dogs, pet owners inadvertently become breeders of this type of mix. Unfortunately, there is little market for mutts, therefore many of these mixed-breed puppies end up in shelters.

Stray dogs also increase the unwanted mutt population. These dogs, who may have been pets themselves at one point in their lives, often mate with other strays or with unsterilized pets who have escaped their homes for brief periods of time. This is why it is so important that all owners spay or neuter their pets as soon as they are old enough for the procedure. Beloved pets escape homes and fenced yards every day. An unfixed male can smell a female in heat from a mile away, and he will find her every time.

In Praise of Mutts

Mixed breeds make incredibly loving pets. Owners of many mixes insist that their dogs have sweeter personalities than any purebred they've ever encountered. The inbreeding and overbreeding of many popular purebred dogs has indeed led to a number of dogs with a range of unsavory temperaments from mildly unpredictable to downright vicious.

Another advantage is that, because mutts are the product of several different dog breeds, they will possess a decreased risk for the afflictions that purebreds may pass on to their offspring. Even designer dogs, whose pedigrees include only two purebreds, possess this quality, which is commonly referred to as hybrid vigor.

A number of designer dog breeds do offer a unique benefit: People who are allergic to most other dogs aren't usually bothered by some designer breeds that have been tailored to be less allergenic. While much depends on the individual breed cross, numerous allergy sufferers have been able to overcome their biggest obstacle to dog ownership by adopting a designer hybrid. Perhaps more so than any other type of dog, a mixed breed is truly one of a kind. While many purebreds are undeniably beautiful, they are also far from original. Think of how boring the world would be if every person looked exactly alike. The same can be said for the canine community. Because a number of breeds are behind mutts, they also inherit a variety of different personality traits. Owning a mutt can be like having several purebred dogs in one!

Because mixed breeds are the product of several different dog breeds, they will possess a decreased risk for the afflictions that purebreds may pass on to their offspring.

Adopting a mixed breed can be even more rewarding than rescuing a purebred dog. As with puppies, purebred dogs are more likely to be adopted than mixed breeds. By adopting a mature mixed breed, you can end up with a friendly, healthy pet and save a life.

A Mixture of Circumstances

Mixed breeds aren't for everyone. If you know in your heart that you want a purebred dog, adopting one is probably the best option for you. Many of us adore our purebreds, each for our own specific reasons. There is nothing wrong with adopting a purebred dog. Every dog adopted is one less homeless animal, and each and every adoption should be applauded.

Perhaps you are searching for a younger dog to adopt, and you want to be confident of what you can expect in the years to come. More than one owner of a mixed breed has been duped by a set of dainty puppy paws that morphed into feet the size of a Clydesdale's as their tiny pups grew into enormous adults. Although purebreds don't always fit their breed standards, most fall within or just outside the general descriptions for their given breed. A purebred Chihuahua will never grow to be the size of a Great Dane.

COMMON BREEDS AND MIXES FOUND IN SHELTERS

Some breeds are more popular than others. Whenever the demand for a certain breed rises, the number of individuals breeding them also increases. Some of these breeders are responsible, ethical people whose primary goal is producing sound dogs for caring pet owners. Other breeders care very little about what happens to their puppies once they are sold. Many of the latter dogs end up in rescues and animal shelters. Here are just a few of the most common breeds and breed mixes found at animal shelters.

Beagles and Hound Mixes

Purebred Beagles are among the most popular members of the AKC's hound group— and among the most common dogs surrendered to shelters. Hound mixes, which are also prevalent shelter residents, include dogs with Beagle, Basset Hound, or Dachshund in their bloodlines. These gentle, friendly dogs can make great family pets. Most have short legs and usually don't require an extreme amount of exercise, although physical activity can help an overweight hound get back into shape.

The primary goal of responsible breeders is to produce sound dogs for caring pet owners.

Breeds Prone to Becoming Overweight

Any dog who eats more calories than he burns will gain weight, but some breeds tend to gain weight more easily than others. These include:

- Basset Hounds
- Beagles
- Cocker Spaniels
- Dachshunds
- French Bulldogs
- Labrador Retrievers
- Pugs
- Shetland Sheepdogs

If you adopt one of these breeds, be sure to feed your pet reasonable food portions and exercise him daily.

Some hounds bay, or howl, if they hear something that catches their attention, but most make poor watchdogs due to their unsuspecting natures.

Many people think hounds are slow learners, especially when it comes to housetraining. Part of the reason for this may be their strong scenting instincts, which can cause them to revisit the scene of a prior housetraining accident even after an owner has thoroughly cleaned the area. General obedience training for hounds should begin indoors so you can establish some success before moving outside where distractions will be more plentiful.

Boxers

Boxers are another common breed found in shelters, largely because many owners do not realize what is involved in owning this breed before they buy one. Boxers are medium-sized, well-muscled dogs with extremely high energy levels. They must be taught to walk properly on a leash. If a Boxer isn't exercised properly, he is especially likely to act out through destructive behavior. Having a strong prey drive, a Boxer may not do well in a home with cats.

Once a Boxer bonds with his new family, he can become

Making Themselves Right at Home

Some breeds are known for adapting to new homes very quickly. Although every dog is different, members of these breeds may be more likely than others to start forming bonds with their new owners immediately:

- Boxers
- English Springer Spaniels
- Greyhounds, particularly retired racing dogs
- Japanese Chin
- Papillons
- Shih Tzu

extremely protective of his loved ones. This makes ongoing training a top priority. Indeed, this is a breed that requires extensive care. Although Boxers have short coats, many owners are surprised by how much they shed; most have to be brushed thoroughly at least twice a week.

Labrador Retrievers and Retriever Mixes

Possibly the most prevalent purebred dog found in shelters, the Labrador Retriever, is one of the most versatile breeds an adoptive owner can choose. Labs are about the same size as a Golden Retriever, only more muscular. Most are great with children, but Labs and Lab mixes can also make great companions for active single people. They are capable and enthusiastic swimmers; some people compare the breed's tail to a rudder when in the water. Many Labs in shelters are overweight because their original owners did not realize just how much exercise they need.

Because they were bred to work with people, these dogs are usually highly responsive to training. Be sure to keep your Lab leashed when outdoors, though, or he may run off to retrieve a bird or other small creature. Even a well-trained dog may succumb to this natural instinct.

Rottweilers

Rottweilers are very intelligent dogs, but they need thorough and consistent training. Weighing in at 100 pounds (45 kg) or more, males Rotties in particular can be extremely hard to handle if training isn't made a top priority. Socialization, too, must be done early and often because the breed has a strong protection instinct. Because this breed bores easily, organized activities like flyball or agility can be practical pastimes for Rottweilers and their owners. This working breed enjoys having something to do and can get into trouble if left alone all day.

A Rottweiler is not a good choice for a first-time pet owner. Ideally, he needs someone who has owned a large breed before and has some experience with obedience training. It is very important that owners establish their household rules from day one with this bright breed, or he will walk (or jump) all over them.

German Shepherds and Shepherd Mixes

German Shepherds are another breed that many people buy impulsively. Once these owners realize that they have bitten off more than they can chew, many of these dogs end up in shelters. Shepherd mixes may include German Shepherd, Collie, or Border Collie in their lineage. Shepherd mixes are usually extremely bright. They are highly trainable but also bore easily, so owners must make training fun.

True to its name, a shepherd will use his natural abilities to herd almost anything—even kids. The dog's intentions may be good, but small children can be hurt during this constant circling. Some shepherds also may nip at ankles in an effort to get their "flock" to move in the direction they desire. Shepherd dogs can make great family pets, provided that owners train them properly and always supervise interactions involving children.

Terrier Mixes

Terrier mixes can include dogs with Bull Terrier, Schnauzer, Scottish Terrier, and many other breeds in their ancestry. The number of breeds that contribute to terrier mixes can seem endless. Virtually any dog with the word "terrier" in his name may be related to

The Most Trainable Breeds

Any dog—purebred or mutt—can learn new tricks. Each dog is different, of course, but some breeds are known for catching on to training extremely quickly. These include:

- Border Collies
- Doberman Pinschers
- German Shepherds
- Golden Retrievers
- Labrador Retrievers
- Poodles
- Rottweilers
- Shetland Sheepdogs
- Welsh Pembroke Corgis

The Truth About Pit Bulls

In recent years, Pit Bulls have earned a reputation for being unequivocally aggressive and untrainable. Some people even think of these amazing dogs as killing machines. Those who know Pit Bulls best say this stereotype is both inaccurate and unfair. Nevertheless, Pit Bulls are a breed of dog commonly found abandoned to shelters and not often adopted.

According to the Humane Society of the United States (HSUS), "Thousands of beloved Pit Bulls live peacefully with families across the country. Pit Bull guardians and animal welfare groups say that it is irresponsible owners and poor breeding—not an inherently vicious nature—that are to blame when Pit Bulls exhibit aggressive behavior toward humans."

Commonly used as therapy dogs, Pit Bulls can make surprisingly good pets. The American Temperament Test Society reports an 83.4 percent pass rate for Pit Bulls. This is higher than the ratings for Australian Shepherds, Beagles, Bulldogs, Collies, Greyhounds, Miniature Poodles, and numerous other breeds.

The HSUS reminds potential adoptive owners, "It's important to remember that every animal is an individual. It's not uncommon for people to be initially apprehensive of Pit Bulls they meet. In fact, many potential adopters might overlook the Pit Bulls at their local animal shelter. When you pass by a Pit Bull, you might be passing by the best dog at the shelter.

"If you're considering adding a new animal to your family, talk to your shelter's adoption counselors, and do some research on your own. Don't exclude a breed or type of dog just because of something you heard or read. That little blocky-headed dog with the goofy grin may be just the friend that you've been waiting for."

your terrier mix. As a group, terriers make very high-energy pets. Even as they reach adulthood, they still seem to behave as if they were in the teenage years of their lives.

Terriers are bright dogs, but they can be extremely stubborn. When trained early and consistently, they learn quickly. When left untrained, they learn quickly how to train their owners instead. Historically used for hunting small ground animals, most terriers have retained a strong hunting instinct. Pets like guinea pigs and gerbils may be in danger in a home with this breed mix. Many terriers get along well with older children, but even young adolescents must be taught how to properly interact with these dogs in order to live successfully with a terrier or terrier mix.

SIZE MATTERS, BUT HOW MUCH?

Perhaps you are drawn to either small or large dogs in particular. Many people prefer pets of a certain size for a variety of reasons. Just as many people like the appearance of a long-haired or short-haired dog better than the other, some people simply prefer the look of either a small or large dog. Owners must be certain, however, that the size of the dog they choose complements their lifestyles and abilities.

Active individuals often enjoy involving their pets in their outdoor activities, such as hiking, biking, or camping. Larger dogs are usually better suited for these pursuits. Conversely, older people may prefer smaller dogs because they are easier to control during training and tend to need less exercise.

If you have limited space, a smaller dog may be the best choice for you. Small dogs typically make the best apartment dwellers. They can even be housetrained to use litter boxes, an added bonus for people who work long hours. Everything about a larger dog is, well, bigger—from their crates and beds to their toys and dishes. Larger dogs also need more space to run around in than do smaller pets.

Bigger dogs are also more expensive. Large dogs eat more food than little ones, and their supplies not only take up more space but also cost more than smaller items. Even vaccines and medications usually cost more for bigger pets because dosages are based on weight.

Smaller dogs are often better choices for people with limited experience with dogs. If you've never owned a dog before, starting with a Samoyed can prove to be more than a little overwhelming for you. Don't be taken in by that cute little Manchester Terrier, though. Small dogs can sometimes be just as demanding of time and training as larger ones. Certainly, adopt the right size dog, but nothing will matter as much as your pet's temperament and personality.

MALE OR FEMALE?

Just as some owners prefer large dogs to small ones (and vice versa), many people will select a dog based on sex alone. Frequently, this partiality is linked to the sex of a formerly cherished pet, and the preference can be deeply ingrained. Yet, similar to human genetics, there are differences that

Both males and females make wonderful pets who are eager to love and be loved.

appear to go along with both x and y canine chromosomes.

As someone who has owned male dogs, I must confess that I think the boys sometimes get a bad rap. Male dogs are often labeled as more aggressive, harder to housetrain, and more destructive than females. Is all of this true? Much depends on the individual dog. In my experience, I have found males to be equally as loving as females, just as quick (or slow—again, depending on the dog) to housetrain, and unfortunately, yes, often a bit more destructive. I have also found them to be less moody and more tolerant of children.

When a male is neutered, as nearly all shelter and rescue dogs are, that dog is far less likely to act aggressively when he reaches sexual maturity due to the decreased level of testosterone in his body. There are many health advantages to spaying or neutering, but for a male dog, many of the benefits are in temperament. Neutered males are easier to train, more tolerant of other males, and far less prone to annoying behaviors like urine marking.

I have also owned female dogs and certainly understand why so many dog lovers adore little girls so much. Females are said to be less distracted during training, less brazen about demanding their owners' attention, and subtler in their defiance—and these are usually accurate assertions. Females tend to be less aggressive with their owners, but they are just as (if not more) domineering with other dogs, particularly other females. They are also by and large craftier about their stubbornness.

Many people wrongly assume that male dogs are the only ones to act out sexually, using a toy or a human's leg, for instance, as an object of immediate gratification. Countless owners report that females perform this act, as well. Early spaying and neutering can help reduce incidences of a sexual nature, but the fact is that this behavior isn't always rooted in sexuality. Often it is an act of dominance—a dog's way of trying to exert authority.

The best thing to do when comparing the sexes is to evaluate your household's present circumstances and even your own personality. There is nothing wrong with preferring one sex to the other. One may indeed be a better choice for you and your family, but both males and females make wonderful pets who are eager to love and be loved.

ADOPTING MORE THAN ONE DOG

Allow your adopted dog some time to acclimate to his new living arrangements before introducing another pet of any kind into the household.

In most cases, it is best to adopt just a single dog at a time. Even if your ultimate goal is to adopt two or more pets, you will

probably make the adoption process easier on both yourself and the dogs by allowing each dog some time to acclimate to the new living arrangements before introducing another pet of any kind into the household.

An exception to this one-pet-at-a-time rule, however, may be if you discover a pair of dogs who were surrendered together. As puppies, most littermates do fine going their separate ways, but older pets who have lived their entire lives together (whether related or not) will likely do best if they are allowed to remain together once adopted. Some shelters and rescues even stipulate that dogs like these must be rehomed as a package deal.

ADOPTING A PREVIOUSLY ABUSED DOG

You may wonder if you have what it takes to care for a dog who was abused by a previous owner. Honestly, the answer depends on many factors, the biggest of which are the individual dog's circumstances and temperament. A younger dog may be able to move on with someone new more easily than an older one or one who has undergone several unsuccessful adoptions following the abusive situation. If the scars from the past abuse are deep and evident in the dog's behavior, this is a definite sign that a lot of hard work lies ahead for both the dog and his new owner.

Additionally, you must consider your own personality and abilities. Will this be your first dog? If so, assuming the care of a previously abused pet may indeed be too much for you. In rare cases, a person completely new to dog ownership can develop just the right rapport with an abused animal, paving the way for successful training and healing. But this isn't the typical scenario. More likely, a dog like this needs someone with experience dealing with animals who have been mistreated in the past.

Most importantly, you must consider whether you have the time and structured lifestyle necessary to train and care for the dog properly. Does your life operate on a dependable schedule? Knowing what to expect each day is enormously reassuring for a previously abused animal. Abused dogs need patient owners who are willing to work hard and ask for help when they need it. Fortunately, many shelters and rescue groups offer follow-up services to assist owners so they won't be going it alone.

The volunteers at your shelter or rescue can help you make the decision of whether you are the right person to offer a previously

Keep in mind that when you adopt a dog, you are committing to caring for him for the rest of his life.

abused dog a new beginning. He, perhaps more than any other dog, deserves a permanent home. If you realize after adopting him that you can't handle it, though, you become just another person who has given up on him, and he must start the process of being rehomed all over again.

Selecting a dog for adoption requires just as much time and effort, if not more so, than choosing a puppy to buy from a breeder, and careful selection can help ensure eventual success. Remember, when you adopt a dog, you are committing to caring for this animal for the rest of his life. Because each breed or mixed breed—each individual dog—is different, you must do your homework before deciding that a particular animal is the one for you. So many wonderful dogs are available for adoption that you are sure to find a pet whose personality and needs match your lifestyle.

Remember that there is no such thing as a perfect dog. Also bear in mind that it can take an adopted dog a bit longer to acclimate to his new home (especially if he has had more than one already). Love can go a long way, but it must be mixed with sensible planning and continuous patience if you want your relationship with your adopted dog to be a happy and lasting one.

4

THE

Adoption Process

K nowing what to expect from the dog adoption process can make the entire experience considerably easier for potential owners. Adopting entails much more than simply deciding to take home a new pet. Whether you go through an animal shelter or a breed rescue to locate your pet, you will have to meet certain criteria before you are allowed to become your chosen dog's new owner.

ADOPTING A DOG FROM A SHELTER OR HUMANE SOCIETY

The top priority of a reputable animal shelter is the well-being of the animals it places. Therefore, shelters ask everyone interested in adopting to fill out a detailed application before being approved for ownership. Nearly all shelters also require prospective adoptive owners to speak with one of their adoption counselors as part of the application process. These volunteers are trained not only to objectively evaluate your suitability for pet ownership, but also to help you decide which dog is the best choice for you.

Be sure to read the shelter's application completely before signing and submitting it. Upon approval, most shelters also require adoptive owners to sign an adoption agreement that outlines both the shelter's and the owner's responsibilities. Common stipulations for owners include agreeing to keep their dogs leashed in public places (with the exception of fenced dog parks) and to always clean up after them. Additionally, this paperwork will state the required adoption fee, any health warranties the shelter provides, and a list of the veterinary services that will be provided prior to adoption. For example, you may expect that the dog you adopt has been tested for heartworm, vaccinated against rabies and distemper, and given a basic deworming. Unless already sterilized when they entered the facility, most shelters dogs are spayed or neutered just prior to being adopted. Some shelters even microchip the pets they place at the time of adoption.

The top priority of a reputable animal shelter is the well-being of the animals they place. Therefore, prospective owners are interviewed and required to meet certain criteria such as having a securely fenced yard to provide daily outdoor exercise.

Common Adoption Requirements

To adopt a dog from a shelter, you must be at least 18 years of age. You will be asked to show a valid form of identification, confirming both your age and physical address. During your interview with the adoption counselor, you also may be asked to provide written proof that you have your landlord's permission to own a dog if you rent your home. Additionally, most shelters ask you to provide two to three personal references.

The counselor will talk to you about your ability and willingness to spend the time and money necessary to care for a pet. Regardless of the age of the dog you adopt, he is likely to need at least some training. Are you prepared to meet this need? Training classes, veterinary care, and even dog food can be expensive these days. The shelter workers need to know that an applicant can handle all the responsibilities involved in dog ownership. Adoption counselors ask a number of routine questions:

• How many people live in your household?
• What are their ages?

- Is everyone in favor of adopting a dog at this time?
- Are there any pets in the household already?

You won't be turned down because you have children, but this information can help the counselor identify those dogs with the proper temperament for your family. Likewise, owning another dog or a cat won't rule you out as an adoptive owner, but it may eliminate a particular dog from your list of potential choices. Remember, volunteers have spent time evaluating the dogs in their care. The counselor's job is creating a healthy match based on this wealth of information.

Some shelters even use detailed owner surveys to create the best possible matches for both the dogs and their new owners. Some of these questions include:

- How much time will your dog spend outdoors?
- On a scale of 1 to 10, how much dog training experience do you have?
- How important is it to you that your dog gets along well with other dogs?
- Do you plan to participate in any organized activities with him?

Your answers to these and other questions give the counselor a

Questions to Ask Shelter or Rescue Volunteers

During the adoption interview process, you will have an opportunity to ask any questions you may have about the dogs you are considering. Here are some things to ask that may help you to make your final decision:

- What is the age (or estimated age) of the dog?
- Does the dog have any medical problems?
- What is the dog's temperament like?
- What is known about the dog's history?
- How many homes has this dog had?
- Is the dog housetrained?
- Is there evidence of any previous obedience training?
- Is there evidence of any previous abuse or neglect?
- Why was the dog surrendered?

You may not get answers to all of these questions. The volunteers may not know a particular detail, or they may be bound by confidentiality laws and therefore unable to share the information. You should always ask these and any other questions you may have in order to make the most informed adoption decision possible.

clear picture of the kind of dog you want and the type of owner you will be.

Once you complete an application, it may be as long as week before you are approved and able to take a dog home. Expect to spend at least a few hours speaking with the shelter staff and meeting different dogs. If the dog you select has not been spayed or neutered yet, this also must be done before homecoming day. You may not even find the dog you're looking for right away. In this case, the shelter can contact you when more dogs become available. Most facilities admit new animals on a regular basis.

What to Look for in a Shelter Dog

Selecting a dog to adopt is about much more than choosing a dog with a particular look. Size and activity level must also be considered, but equally important is a dog's disposition. For adoption to be successful, you must select a dog whose temperament matches your expectations.

If you're like most adoptive owners, you want a friendly dog. To find out which dogs fit this description, walk along the

The amount of one-on-one time spent with the dog you are considering is important in deciding if he is indeed the right pet for you.

kennels and make a mental note of those who come forward immediately to greet you. Dogs showing signs of shyness or fear in the shelter can be difficult to assess. A shelter can be a scary place, especially for a newcomer. Some of these animals may have fine temperaments, but it can be difficult to predict with any certainty how these dogs will act once outside the shelter environment. If a dog growls or lunges at you, though, you should rule him out unless you are an experienced handler or trainer who can deal with serious behavior problems.

Just as you should be leery of dogs who are slow to warm up to you, you also should consider overexcitement a cause for concern. Dogs who do everything short of cartwheels when you approach them may be hyperactive. If you plan to spend every minute of your day with your adopted dog, this should not be a problem for you. If you must leave your dog at home when you go to work each day, though, this may not be the best choice for you.

A dog who shows a moderate amount of interest in interacting with you is usually ideal. Look for a dog who comes over to greet you calmly, happily wagging his tail. Once you have had a chance to get marginally acquainted, ask if you can visit with him somewhere without a barrier. Most shelters have a quiet place for owners interested in particular animals to spend some time getting to know them. This one-on-one time spent with the dog you are considering is important in deciding if he is indeed the right pet for you.

Watch the dog closely as the shelter volunteer opens his kennel and leashes him before showing you to the more private area. Does he readily accept the leash or start resisting it the moment he sees it? Does he pull once the leash is attached? If you don't mind working on this issue, his reaction might not be a huge concern for you. Remember, temperament is paramount. But if you prefer a dog who already knows how to walk on a leash properly, this could be a disadvantage with this specific animal.

While in the "get-to-know-you" area, ask the volunteer about the dog's behavior and experiences at the shelter thus far. The reason for doing this is twofold. First, it provides you with some additional insight into the dog's temperament. Second, it gives

It's natural to feel excited about meeting the dog you hope will become your new pet. You may also feel a little nervous. It's very important, though, that you remain calm and focused at this point in the adoption process. Animals, particularly dogs, can sense when a person is anxious. This can lead them to act in ways that are out of character for them. You want to make the dog you are meeting feel as comfortable as possible, so that he can relax in your presence. This is the only way to get an accurate impression of his temperament and personality. If you worry, you may forget something important in your excitement, so bring a written list of your questions for the volunteers. I also recommend using a voice recorder to capture their answers. This will help you weigh all available information when deciding if this dog is the one for you.

you the opportunity to see how the dog responds to being around people. Does he sit quietly but eagerly awaiting interaction while you and the volunteer speak to each other? Or does he jump up on you or bark, demanding your attention? The former scenario is highly preferable.

Although it can be tempting to fall in love with a dog who takes an instant liking to you, you must also consider how he responds to others. This is an important reason to involve everyone from your household in the adoption process. Is he as wild about your spouse as he is about you? Even if you live alone, I suggest bringing a friend or two along with you so that you can see how the dog reacts to a variety of people.

Avoid relying entirely on details provided by the dog's original owner. This information may or may not be truthful because so many people who surrender their pets lie about things that they fear will keep the animals from being adopted. Instead, observe the dog and draw your own conclusions about him from his behavior.

Once the dog comes to you, gently stroke his head and back. Does he welcome being touched and appear to enjoy being petted? A steady tail wag is usually a reliable sign of this. Next, slowly lift and handle each of his paws. How does he react? Many dogs, especially those who aren't used to having their nails trimmed, will pull away when someone touches their feet. This isn't a deal breaker by any means, but a dog who growls or tries to nip may be showing you that he has fear-aggression issues. The dog needn't lie down and show you his belly right away (although if he does, it's a wonderful sign of a submissive temperament), but he also shouldn't challenge you in any way.

If the dog's file says he knows a handful of basic commands, this is a great time to try them out. In a firm but pleasant tone, tell him to sit or lie down, and watch how quickly he complies. The number of commands a dog knows is far less important than his willingness to abide by your instructions. If the dog follows commands from you, a virtual stranger, you can take this as an excellent sign of trainability.

If something doesn't seem right about the dog, keep looking. Even if you can't articulate the problem, follow your instincts. When you adopt a dog, you commit to caring for this animal for the rest of his life—you should feel confident, not ambivalent, about your choice.

ADOPTING A DOG FROM A BREED RESCUE

Adopting a dog from a breed rescue group is in many ways very similar to adopting a pet from an animal shelter, but there are some differences. Like a shelter, a rescue group will ask you to fill out a detailed application, the key word being detailed. Breed rescue organizations have a reputation for being extremely thorough. They expect a lot from their adoptive owners because they want their dogs to find permanent, loving homes. Remember, the dog you may end up adopting has already lost at least one home.

The breed rescue's adoption agreement will be more comprehensive than that used by shelters. In addition to asking you to care for your adopted dog and keep him safe, a breed rescue will ask that you pledge to never transfer ownership of the dog to anyone—not even a family member— but instead surrender the dog back to the rescue in the event that you can no longer care for him. Other details of this agreement can vary, but some require owners to provide the animal with a specific amount of exercise each day or to promise to never transport the dog in the back of a pickup truck.

If you live with other people, you must consider if they are ready for dog adoption. Ideally, the entire household should participate in the decision-making process.

Whereas a shelter may ask questions about your home and lifestyle, a rescue group will schedule a home visit before approving your adoption application. Practical amenities such as a fenced yard are considered a plus, but don't be surprised if the visiting volunteer measures the height of the enclosure, especially if the dog you will be adopting is a taller breed. Your home need not be fancy to impress a breed rescue, though. The purpose of this inspection is not to ensure that the dogs go to affluent homes or even perfectly kept ones. A neat and clean home is a definite advantage, but a little dust won't hurt your chances of approval one bit. The volunteers simply want to confirm that the home the dog goes to is indeed the one you described.

In addition to asking you to take proper care of your adopted dog and keep him safe, a breed rescue will require that you pledge never to transfer ownership of him but instead surrender him back to the rescue if you can no longer care for him.

Another purpose of the home visit is to provide the rescue volunteer with a chance to meet your entire family, including your children and any pets you already have. If your spouse and kids can't make the appointment because of other commitments, this may lead the rescue volunteer to wonder if a dog might get lost in the shuffle of your family's hectic life, which is an understandable concern.

It can take a rescue organization a couple of weeks or longer to approve your application. Try to be patient during this time. Because rescues can vary so dramatically in size, there may be just one person available to go over your application, check your references, and come to your home.

Once the breed rescue approves your adoption application, you can then begin meeting dogs in need of new homes. Unlike a shelter, where you can meet all the dogs available in a single day, meeting rescue dogs can be a bit more time consuming, if for no other reason than geography. A dog you meet today may be staying with a volunteer in one town, but the dog who becomes available next week might be staying with another rescue worker 5, 10, or even 20 miles away.

What to Look for in a Rescue Dog

Use the same criteria for selecting a rescue dog as you would for choosing a dog at the shelter. Look for a calm, friendly, and well-adjusted animal. If you think a particular dog might be the right one for you, ask as many questions as possible and listen carefully to all the answers. Since most breed rescues can tell you so much more about their dogs than shelters can, take advantage of this wealth of information. You may be able to tell right away if a dog isn't right for you, but being certain that another dog is the right match can take a bit longer.

Just as every person in your household should be present for the rescue volunteer's visit to your home, your entire family should participate in the process of selecting the dog you adopt. If you are concerned that younger family members may fall in love with the first dog they meet—and be disappointed if he doesn't turn out to be the right dog for your family—you can plan the first meeting for the adults only. Once you have chosen a dog that you think is the right one, you can then arrange for the kids to meet this potential pet. Do not make a final decision, however, until everyone has had a chance to offer an opinion about the dog.

Most importantly, don't feel rushed to adopt any dog. After all the hoops you may feel you've been asked to jump through, you might want to move through the selection process as quickly as possible. You may even feel pressure from a rescue volunteer to make a choice. Remember, though, you will be living with the dog you choose for the duration of his life. Take as much time as you need to make your final decision.

WHAT TO DO IF YOU'RE TURNED DOWN

If the animal shelter or rescue group declines your application for adoption, ask a volunteer to explain why you were not deemed a suitable owner at this time. Listen to the explanation, and try not to be defensive. It may be that your present circumstances simply aren't right for adoption, or it may be that you aren't the right match for the breed you have chosen. If your situation changes, apply again down the road, or consider a different breed that better suits your current lifestyle. The dog of your dreams may be waiting for you in another breed rescue or at another time.

Scheduling Your Dog's Homecoming

Most animal shelters and rescue organizations require adoptive owners to plan a time to pick up their new pets. In most situations, dogs are sterilized just prior to going home with their new families. This gives the new owners valuable time to prepare for the homecoming. Even if the shelter or rescue tells you that you can take the dog you choose right away, ask to schedule this important step. Having all the necessary supplies—food, dishes, a crate—already on hand will help make your dog's transition into your home a smoother one.

Chapter 5

PREPARING
for Your New Arrival

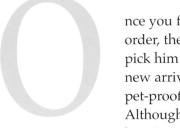

nce you find the dog you want to adopt and the paperwork is all in order, the next step is scheduling his homecoming. Before you can pick him up, however, you will have to prepare your home for the new arrival. You must shop for all the items your dog will need, pet-proof his surroundings, and arrange for his veterinary care. Although this sounds like an arduous to-do list, you will have it done in no time if you take it one step at a time.

SUPPLIES

It can be tempting to fill your pet store shopping cart with all sorts of extras to pamper your newly adopted pet, but I suggest limiting yourself to the following items, at least for your initial supply run. You are already giving your dog the gift he needs most—a loving and permanent home. Hopefully, the two of you have already had a chance to get acquainted, but the next week or two should be spent getting to know each other better and beginning your new household routine. As you spend more time with your dog, any additional items he might need will become clear to you.

I always advise dog owners against making impulsive purchases. Trendy items may seem cute or fun at first but many are a waste of money. If you worry that you may be overlooking something important for your pet, check with your shelter or rescue volunteer.

Collar and Leash

The first two items you will need for your adopted dog are a collar and leash. Some shelters and rescues send adopted dogs home with a basic collar and leash set; others do not. The worst time to find out that your dog won't be given these necessary items is when you go to pick him up, so ask about this when you schedule your dog's homecoming. Pick up a second set either way, though, because these everyday accessories will need to be washed from time to time.

Leather and nylon are versatile choices for collars and leashes because both materials

Common Scents

When you make arrangements to adopt your new pet, ask the volunteers at the shelter or rescue organization if you can leave a toy or other item with him until he comes home with you. If he has a favorite possession already—a bed or blanket, for instance—he may be allowed to take it with him when he leaves. Because this item will have the scent of the shelter or foster home on it, it may be comforting for your dog to keep it with him as he gets used to his new home with you. If the item comes from you, it also can help your new dog get used to your scent so that your home may seem familiar to him the first time he enters it.

are strong and lightweight. Chains, however, are too heavy for smaller dogs or those with delicate necks. Prong collars, shock collars, or choke chains should never be used on any dog, no matter what his size or breed because these items inflict pain. Avoid any item that causes your adopted dog pain or discomfort, including spray collars that emit strong, unpleasant scents as behavior deterrents. Positive reinforcement, such as praise, for good behavior is not only more humane but is also far more effective than any kind of punishment for undesirable behavior.

To fit your dog for his collar, measure his neck with the tape just loose enough for you to slide two fingers underneath it. If the collar is too tight, it can hurt him. Also, I recommend collars with breakaway technology. This innovative feature will protect your pet by releasing him if his collar ever becomes caught on another object. If the collar is too loose, it can slip off. This too can be dangerous. If your dog escapes the safety of his collar—and therefore his leash, too—when he is outdoors, he can become lost, get hit by an automobile, or have any number of other devastating things happen to him.

Some dogs have an uncanny knack for slipping out of collars. For them, body harnesses can be a better option. Conventional harnesses wrap around your dog's body in two places: both in front of his chest and underneath it. Like a collar, you must get an accurate measurement in order for a harness to fit your dog correctly. Using the same two-finger strategy as for a collar, measure your dog's girth, which is the circumference of his upper chest just behind his front legs. Avoid relying on weight ranges when selecting a body harness because this information can be misleading. Dogs with very different chest measurements can weigh the same amount.

If your dog pulls, I recommend using a head harness. This special harness, typically made of nylon, wraps gently around your dog's muzzle and moves his head downward whenever he begins pulling. A dog cannot continue pulling in this position. If there is one downside to using a head harness, it may be that to some people it looks a little like a muzzle. It is not, however, anything of the kind. Dogs can open their mouths to eat, drink, and even bite while wearing a head harness.

Like your dog's collar, his leash should be the right size for his stature. It should allow him to walk comfortably alongside you, but it should not be so long as to allow him to venture into the street. If your dog displays a tendency to gnaw on his lead while walking, it may be smart to buy a leather leash. Leather will fare better than nylon while you train him away from this behavior.

Once your dog has been properly trained to walk on a conventional leash, I recommend investing in a retractable lead. Owning this extendable lead is like having several different leashes in one. You can lengthen the lead to up to 16 feet (about 5 m) or more when you are walking your dog in the park or other areas without traffic, and then retract it to as little as 4 feet (1 m) or any length in between whenever necessary. The accommodating design also makes this type of leash ideal for teaching your dog to come to you when called. Most retractable leads are housed within lightweight plastic handles, many of which are ergonomically designed for a comfortable grip. Some even come with refillable containers of bags for cleaning up after your pet.

Be sure to purchase the right size lead for your dog. A large dog should never be walked on a retractable lead made for a

The first two items you will need for your adopted dog are a collar and leash. You will need these to ensure his safety when you bring him home from the shelter or rescue.

smaller pet; the line simply isn't strong enough. Check the label for information on weight limits. Also, check the line of your dog's lead from time to time to make sure the cord is in proper shape. If any area has frayed, the integrity of the lead has been compromised, and it should be replaced at once.

Food and Water Bowls

Every dog needs a set of food and water bowls. I recommend buying two sets so that you always have a clean pair ready when the other set is in the dishwasher. Speaking of the dishwasher, many plastic and ceramic dishes are not dishwasher safe. Plastic also can cause a condition in dogs called plastic dish nasal dermatitis, a sometimes painful inflammation of the skin that can also lead to pigment loss in the dog's nose and lips. Plastic is also extremely vulnerable to chewing. Ceramic stands up better to teeth, but these bowls usually shatter if dropped or knocked across a tile floor. And because currently there are no regulations for lead content in dishes made for pets, ceramic can be even more dangerous to your dog than plastic.

Stainless steel bowls are the best choice. They can be washed easily by hand or in the dishwasher. They also won't break no matter how many times you drop them. More importantly, they are completely safe for your dog, provided that you wash them regularly. (Nothing invites bacteria better than merely topping off your pet's food and water each day.)

Stainless steel food bowls are the best choice for your dog.

If you adopt a large breed dog like a Weimaraner, don't buy him bowls that are housed in a raised table. Although this item may appear to make eating more comfortable for a bigger dog, eating in an upright position can increase his chances of suffering from a serious condition called gastric dilatation-volvulus (GDV). Commonly called bloat or stomach torsion, GDV is a life-threatening emergency that causes air to become trapped inside a dog's stomach and cuts off blood flow to other organs.

Smaller breeds face a decreased risk for GDV, but perhaps even more interesting is that mixed breeds are also less susceptible to suffering from bloat than most purebreds. A study conducted by the University of Purdue calculated a ratio for the likelihood of a particular breed developing the problem compared to a mixed breed dog. Your Weimaraner is 19.3 times more likely to experience bloat than a mixed-breed dog. The narrower and deeper the dog's chest, the more this number goes up. A Great Dane, for instance, is 41.4 times more likely to suffer from this problem than a mixed-breed.

Food

Of course, once you've picked out your dog's bowls, you will need some food to put in them. Numerous types of dog food can be found at your local pet supply store. You may even decide you would like to cook for your new pet. For now, though, the most practical choice is to feed your dog the same food he has been eating while living at the shelter or staying with his foster family. To prevent stomach upset, changing a dog from one food to another should always be done gradually, but I suggest postponing any dietary modifications until your adopted dog has had a chance to adjust to his new life with you. By limiting the number of changes he must deal with at once, you increase his chances for a successful transition into your home and family.

Crate and Safety Gates

If you plan to crate train your adopted dog, you will need to have this item before you bring your new pet home. Once again, size is one of the most important factors in selecting a crate or kennel for your pet. A crate should be large enough to allow your dog to lie down, stand up, and turn around while inside it. If the crate is too big, however, he may be tempted to use one end of it as a bathroom.

Hard plastic crates, as well as wire models, are available at most pet supply stores. Each style comes with its own advantages. Which is best for you and your dog depends on your individual circumstances.

Dogs who began their lives in puppy mills can be especially frightened of being inside a crate again. A better option for these dogs is a safety gate.

In many ways, a plastic crate is the most practical choice. Plastic crates are easy to assemble and disassemble, and they offer a dog a more private environment than wire models. They also are allowed on most airplanes, an important consideration if you plan to travel with your adopted pet.

If your dog is younger or tends to chew, however, a wire crate will be more resistant to destruction. Wire also can be a smarter choice for dogs who enjoy being involved in the activity of their households. If your adopted dog wants to be with you all the time, the open design of a wire crate can make him feel more a part of your family. For a dog with this type of personality, place the crate in a high-traffic spot in your home—in the kitchen, for instance.

To make sure your dog's crate is a comfortable place for him to spend time, be sure to purchase a crate liner. This cushion-like item should match the interior dimensions of the kennel and be at least a few inches thick. Liners are available in a wide range of fabrics, including warm fleece and smooth microfiber. Some are even reversible, offering dogs two different textures. Like a pet bed, a liner should be machine-washable because it will need to be laundered periodically.

Crates are useful not only for housetraining your dog but also for keeping him safe. I place my dogs in their crates whenever I go grocery shopping so they cannot escape through the door when I am carrying my bags inside the house. Crates also keep dogs from getting into mischief when their owners cannot watch them.

If your dog will be sleeping in his crate at night, you may

want to invest in a second one to place in another area of your home so you don't have to carry the crate up a set of stairs or move it to a more convenient spot each time you place him in it. And as long as you only have one dog, buying two crates instead of just one shouldn't be too expensive either.

Even with all their advantages, though, crates aren't for all dogs. Dogs who began their lives in puppy mills can be especially frightened of being inside a crate again. A better option for these dogs is a safety gate. Whether you opt for a portable gate that can be set up in any doorway of your home or a swing-style model that can contain your dog to a particular room, a gate can be a wise investment, even if you use a crate as well. Safety gates can be found at most pet supply stores, as well as in the baby-care sections of most department stores.

Bed

If you are adopting a young dog, you may want to hold off on investing in a bed for him until he is both housetrained and past the teething stage. This doesn't mean that he won't need a comfortable place to sleep in the meantime, however. Even if your adopted dog is a bit older, you may want to make sure that he isn't a voracious chewer before buying this item. An old folded blanket or comforter can serve as a fine substitute until your dog is ready for more plush accommodations.

If your dog is unlikely to soil or gnaw a pet bed, this item should top your shopping list. Pet beds are available in a wide array of fabrics and styles. You can find one to match nearly any

What Size Crate Does My Adopted Dog Need?	
Recommended Crate Size	Breed or Breed Mix
Extra small: approximately 18 to 22 inches (46 to 56 cm)	Small Terrier Mixes, Toy Poodle, Yorkshire Terrier
Small: approximately 24 inches (61 cm)	Dachshund, Shih Tzu
Medium: approximately 30 inches (76 cm)	Medium Terrier Mixes, Miniature Poodle, Small Hound Mixes
Intermediate: approximately 36 inches (91 cm)	Beagle, Cockapoo, Medium Hound Mixes
Large: approximately 42 inches (107 cm)	Boxer, Bulldog, Large Hound Mixes, Large Terrier Mixes
Extra large: approximately 48 inches (122 cm)	German Shepherd, Golden Retriever, Labrador Retriever, Labradoodle, Shepherd Mixes, Standard Poodle

No matter what type of bed your dog uses, place it where he can be near you. This is especially important during his first few days in his new home.

room, but more important than this is that you select one that is the right size for your dog. It should be just a little longer than your dog when he is lying stretched out fully. Your dog may prefer to curl up when he sleeps, but he should have enough room if he feels like sprawling out.

Wooden shavings have been used for years to stuff pet beds. Many dogs find shavings to be quite comfy, but cedar-scented shavings can be tough on many dogs' noses. Shredded foam and even memory foam (like the material used to make mattresses for people) are excellent alternatives. You may even find special orthopedic foam for older or arthritic dogs.

Be sure the bed you choose has a removable, machine-washable cover. Even if your dog is reliably housetrained, his bed is bound to need cleaning from time to time. A hidden zipper is also a smart feature to keep your dog from chewing it.

No matter what type of bed your dog uses, place it where he can be near you. Although some trainers advise against allowing dogs to sleep on their owners' beds, many encourage owners of adopted dogs to let their pets sleep in their bedrooms at night. If your dog will be sleeping in his own bed, this makes the bedroom an ideal location for it. If he will be sleeping in his crate, you may wish to place his dog bed in another room where the two of you spend a lot of time together.

Grooming Supplies

Certain dogs need to be groomed more often than others, but all dogs need the same basic tools to keep them looking and feeling their best. You don't need to spend a lot of money for items of good quality, but that old saying about getting what you pay for is true to a certain degree. You needn't spend an arm and a leg for a set of professional grooming shears, for example, but a metal comb will last a lot longer than one made of plastic. An expensive shampoo may not get your dog any cleaner than a low-priced brand, but if you must use more of the cheaper brand, its high water content may make it more economical in the end to opt to spend the few extra dollars.

Even short-haired dogs need to be brushed regularly. Brushing removes dirt, dead hair, and other debris from your pet's coat. Soft-bristled brushes usually work fine for short-haired dogs, but a dog with longer hair needs either a pin or slicker style brush in order for you to reach his skin while brushing him. Many owners also find a fine-toothed comb useful, both for checking their dogs for fleas and for making sure they didn't miss any knots during the brushing process.

Whether you take your dog on daily hikes in the woods or he spends the majority of his time indoors, he will need to be bathed occasionally. Human hair products must never be used on dogs. The pH levels of their skin and hair differ drastically from a human's, and a dog's skin can become dry and itchy if his owners use their own products on him. A great way to lengthen the time between your dog's shampoos is by giving him regular sponge baths.

Your dog's toenails will need to be trimmed at least once or twice a month. Although many groomers offer this service, it is practical to pick up your own set of nail clippers. If your dog is on the smaller side, a pair of canine nail scissors may do the job. Many owners of larger dogs, though, prefer either guillotine or pliers-style trimmers because bigger nails tend to be harder and thicker. Be sure to choose the right size nail clipper for your pet.

If your adopted dog balks at the idea of having his nails cut, consider using a grinding tool instead. This rotary device both shortens and smoothes nails instead of cutting them. By using a nail grinder, you can avoid cutting into the quick—a mistake that can leave your dog even more fearful of pedicures. A special trimmer electronically designed to sense the location of the nail bed may also be helpful for this purpose. This amazing device can literally sense the blood vessels within the nail and alert you when you get too close to them with the clipper. Both this item and most rotary tools are battery-powered, making them easy to use virtually anywhere.

Finally, don't forget to pick up some ear cleaning solution for your new pet. Whether he has long pendulous ears or shorter upright ears, you will need to clean them about once every week or two to prevent infection. Ear cleansers can be purchased at most pet supply stores, or you can make your own by mixing equal parts vinegar and water.

Toys

All dogs need toys. Talk to the volunteers at the shelter or rescue about which types of toys your adopted dog likes best. Toys help dogs pass the time. They also can be extremely useful in training your new pet and steering him away from problem behaviors. A dog with numerous toys that his owner rotates regularly is far less likely to engage in destructive behaviors like inappropriate chewing and excessive barking.

If your dog is still teething or is a voracious chewer, be sure to provide him with plenty of durable chew toys. Even if your adopted dog is older, he still may enjoy a flavored chew bone like the ones Nylabone makes. A toy that can be stuffed with yummy treats can also win over a discriminating dog.

Start with a few different items, and see for yourself what your adopted dog likes best. Many dogs enjoy balls and plush toys that squeak, but often a dog will favor one type of toy over all others. When your adopted dog first comes to live with you, having a favorite item with him can help make him feel more at home. To keep him interested in playing, though, introduce something new from time to time, even if he seems to prefer an old standard. He just might discover a new favorite toy in the process.

My Bag of Tricks

I keep a bag of new dog toys hidden away for those occasions when I want to give each of my dogs a special treat. Every now and then when I stop at the pet supply store to pick up dog food, I buy a few new items to add to my stash. Sometimes I go with tried and true playthings, like a Nylabone and a rope toy, always favorites in our house. Other times I try something new. In addition to rotating my dogs' toys regularly, I use this bag of tricks to help keep playtime fun and exciting for my pets. If a particular toy isn't well received, there's always another just waiting to be let out of the bag.

All dogs need toys. Aside from providing activity and exercise, they can be extremely useful in training your new pet and steering him away from problem behaviors.

Remember, some toys are only fun when used with a playmate. Flying disks, for example, require two players: a human thrower and a canine receiver. When you play with your adopted dog, you utilize toys as tools for bonding with him. That favorite blue ball becomes even more fun when your dog has someone to fetch it for.

Identification

Many dogs living in shelters across the country are there because they became lost. Without a reliable piece of identification, a lost dog's chances of being returned to his owner drop significantly. A lot of people think their dogs will never get lost, but countless owners are proven wrong about this every day. Some travel great distances, ending up in shelters miles (sometimes even entire states) away from their original homes. These are the lucky ones. Left to run free, a dog can be hit by a vehicle or attacked by a wild animal. Sadly, many owners never learn the fates of their lost pets.

The quickest and easiest means of providing a dog with identification is purchasing an ID tag for him. Engravable tags can be made at most pet supply stores and are extremely inexpensive. Be sure to include your complete contact information, such as your name, address, and phone number with area code. And don't forget to attach your dog's tag to his collar. A tag can only help identify your pet if he is wearing it when he becomes lost.

So, what if your dog isn't wearing his collar when he escapes? A more permanent form of identification is necessary in this situation, as well as if your dog is ever stolen. Microchipping has become an incredibly popular safety precaution for these very reasons. A veterinarian can microchip your dog during a routine appointment. The process is no more painful than a shot, and unlike tattooing—the most popular method of permanent identification in the past—your dog does not need anesthesia to be microchipped. The microchip itself is about the size of a grain of rice. When scanned by a handheld device used by most veterinarians and animal shelters worldwide, the transponder reveals a unique number linked to your dog in the company's registry.

Be sure to update your contact information if it changes so that you can be reunited with your pet should he ever become lost or stolen.

The easiest means of providing a dog with identification is purchasing an ID tag for him. A tag can help identify your pet if he is wearing it when he becomes lost.

Numerous shelters are jumping on the microchipping bandwagon, chipping each dog before he is placed with a new owner. Because the practice has also become popular with owners in recent years, I suggest asking your shelter or rescue if your adopted dog has already been microchipped before scheduling an appointment.

There is another type of tag every dog needs: a dog license; most states require that owners license their dogs. Call your local city hall to find out exactly what paperwork you need to bring with you when applying for registration. This typically includes a current rabies certificate. Bring along confirmation that your adopted dog has been spayed or neutered as well because the licensing fee for sterilized pets is usually less than the amount charged for intact animals.

Even with a microchip, your dog still needs a license and an identification tag. One form of ID is not a substitute for the other. If you and your pet are ever separated, these tags can help the two of you reunite as quickly as possible. And this is, after all, the primary goal of any form of canine identification.

Clothing

Aside from these essentials, another item you may wish to consider if you live in a colder climate is a sweater or coat for your dog. Many dogs love being outdoors, regardless of the season. Mine especially enjoy playing in snow. I have to virtually drag them back inside, even during New England's most frigid temperatures. Some may argue that larger breeds or those with heavier coats of their own don't need cold weather clothing, but seeing my Cocker Spaniels shiver (and still insist on staying outdoors) was enough to encourage me to invest in two different canine winter accessories: coats and boots.

To determine your dog's coat size, measure him from collar to tail. For a long time, I preferred sweaters to coats; the cutesy designs of most coats I'd seen appeared to be high on fashion but lacking in warmth. I find that fleece coats, however, provide even more warmth than many sweaters. They also aren't as susceptible to snags from claws and teeth.

Protecting the Paws

One of the contradictions I have observed in many dogs is their affection for water—on their own terms, that is. My dog, Molly, will actually pout if I draw a bath for anyone in the house other than her. She needs absolutely no coaxing when it is her turn to get into the tub. (My first Cocker had to be bribed with luncheon meat, mind you.) Molly also really enjoys swimming in the summer. On a rainy day, however, just the thought of getting her feet wet is enough to make her pull to go back inside as soon as we set out for her walk. If your adopted dog is anything like Molly, consider purchasing a set of doggy boots. Try them on in the store to ensure both size and comfort. Some

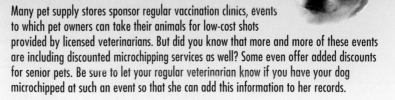

One-Stop Shopping: Microchipping

Many pet supply stores sponsor regular vaccination clinics, events to which pet owners can take their animals for low-cost shots provided by licensed veterinarians. But did you know that more and more of these events are including discounted microchipping services as well? Some even offer added discounts for senior pets. Be sure to let your regular veterinarian know if you have your dog microchipped at such an event so that she can add this information to her records.

dogs will not tolerate having their feet confined within boots, but many others wear them with ease.

Another problem most owners overlook is their dogs' continual exposure to the harshest outdoor surfaces. In cold weather this may be snow and ice—or worse, salt. In the summer it may be hot pavement or prickly rocks and gravel. Applying paw wax can help protect your dog's paws and pads from these virtually unavoidable elements. In addition to providing a protective layer to ward off abrasions, burning, drying, and cracking, this unique product also gives your dog better traction when walking on ice. Although paw wax will not keep his feet dry, it will act as an invisible boot by getting between your dog's vulnerable pads and any surface they touch. You can find this product at most pet supply stores.

INDOOR AND OUTDOOR DOG-PROOFING

Bringing a dog into your home can be a lot like adding a human child to your household. Dogs, both young and old, can get into trouble if reasonable safety precautions aren't taken. Some of these changes not only protect your new pet but also protect your belongings from possible harm.

If dog-proofing your entire home seems like a colossal (or even impossible) task, I recommend starting by tackling a single room. If just one room in your home has been made safe for your adopted dog, he can hang out there while you work on making additional areas more pet friendly. If you will be housetraining him, choosing a room without carpeting is a smart step.

Begin by picking up as many things off the floor as you can. Shoes and children's toys look a lot like dog toys to many canines. This is especially important if your dog is still teething. That beautiful wicker basket you found at the flea market may work great for storing newspapers and magazines, but it won't be nearly as attractive (or functional) after your dog shreds it along with its contents. The range of items a voracious chewer will accept as impromptu chew toys may surprise you. When my son Alec had his braces removed earlier this year, his orthodontist advised us to keep his retainer and soccer mouth guard in a safe place where our dogs wouldn't be able to reach them. He told us that, oddly enough, dogs appeared to be drawn to these items and that he'd had to replace several for other dog-owning patients. When my mother's Cocker Spaniel, Savannah, was a puppy, she completely destroyed several pairs of eyeglass frames as well as a large sand cast sculpture of a fellow Cocker. To a teething dog, no item is sacred.

In addition to ruining your possessions, your dog can also hurt himself if certain items are left out for him to investigate. Plants can be particularly dangerous, but low-lying electrical cords and open wastebaskets are also accidents just waiting to send the two of you to the emergency vet. Unplug and spray any cords that cannot be raised out of the way with a pet-safe, bitter-tasting repellent, and block access to any open electrical outlets by inserting safety plugs. Use your garbage disposal to discard food items, and place bones and any other sharp objects (like disposable razors) directly into your outdoor trash container. Even household recyclables can pose a hazard to a curious dog; I always tie plastic bags into a knot before tossing them into my recycling bin, and I place aluminum cans and their tops in securely closed recyclable containers.

If your dog can reach your kitchen counter, place any food items that normally go there inside your cupboards or in a pantry closet until you are confident that he won't help himself. Even items that wouldn't make your dog sick in

Dogs, both young and old, can get into trouble if reasonable safety precautions aren't taken. For example, never leave your dog in a room with open doors or windows.

Many flowers and plants are poisonous to dogs. To find out if a particular plant is safe, check with your veterinarian.

moderate quantities can cause life-threatening problems if consumed in large amounts. Certain breads, for instance, expand extensively once eaten. This can lead to constipation and even intestinal blockages. Other foods—including chocolate, onions, and macadamia nuts—should never be eaten by dogs, not even in small amounts.

Never leave your dog in a room with open doors or windows. If the weather is warm, place child safety bars in your windows before opening them, or turn on the air conditioner instead. Many dogs can jump or chew through screens in record time. If your dog escapes a room on the first floor of your home, he could become lost. If he pushes himself through a window screen on the second floor, he could fall to his death.

Remember to dog-proof your home both inside and out. Fenced yards make great play areas for dogs, but never leave a dog unattended outdoors. An adept digger can make his way under a fence before many of us could manage the task with a shovel.

If your home is landscaped, be sure that any gardening products you use are safe for use around pets. Known for its fine texture and sweet smell, cocoa mulch is a big no-no for dog owners because it contains the same two ingredients that make chocolate toxic to pets: theobromine and caffeine. Many flowers and plants are also poisonous to dogs, such as daffodils, tulips, and rhododendrons just to name a few. To find out if a particular plant is safe, check with your veterinarian. Many vets will provide their clients with lists of plants that are safe to keep around pets.

If you have a pool, never allow your dog near this area unsupervised. Although most dogs can swim, no animal can tread water indefinitely. Your dog can drown before you even realize that he has fallen in. Even a hot tub can pose a drowning danger to a small dog.

Clean up any vehicle spills in your garage or on your driveway. These chemicals can be deadly if lapped up by your pet. Antifreeze is especially hazardous because it has a sweet taste that many dogs love. When buying antifreeze, look for pet-safe products containing propylene glycol instead of ethylene glycol.

Finally, don't forget to keep your dog's potty spot clean. Numerous diseases can be spread through fecal matter. As soon as your dog eliminates, praise him and dispose of any solid waste. Not only does this make your yard look and smell better, it also helps to keep your dog healthy. Always clean up after your pet when he eliminates during walks, too. In addition to being the conscientious thing to do, it is also the law.

FINDING A VETERINARIAN

Your dog's veterinarian is much more than just the person who treats your pet when he gets sick. A vet is also your best resource for helping your pet stay healthy. At one time, the veterinarian's role in pet care was limited to medical issues, but today vets and animal owners act as partners in creating healthy lifestyles for pets. Got a question about your dog's diet? Ask his vet. Not sure how to clip your dog's toenails? Watch carefully as his vet gives you a demonstration. Worried that your dog will never become housetrained? Get some pointers from his vet.

Finding a veterinarian to treat your dog isn't a difficult job, but choosing the best person for your pet can seem a bit challenging at first. Many suburban areas now have at least two or three different veterinary hospitals; populous cities usually have even more. How do you know which vet is the right one? I recommend relying on word of mouth as a starting point. Ask your friends and neighbors whom they use. If you adopt a dog from a local shelter or rescue, ask the volunteers whom they recommend. Receiving the same name from more than one person is a good sign.

Make a list of the vets recommended to you, and visit each hospital's website. Most have one these days. You will be able to get answers to many of your questions this way. Location, operating hours, and basic policies are usually posted online. You also may be able to find a list of prices for the most common services.

Once you have chosen a veterinarian you would like to consider further, stop by the hospital to request a meeting with the vet and a tour of the facility. You mustn't expect the staff to fit you in right on the spot, but most hospitals are happy to show you around at a mutually convenient time. By dropping by unannounced to make this appointment, though, you will get to witness an example of a typical day at the hospital. Watch how the employees interact with canine patients and their owners while you wait to speak with a receptionist. The staff members should be pleasant, even if the work load is high and the waiting room is full. And they should all possess an obvious love for animals.

The facilities should be clean and well organized, but they need not be fancy. Don't get lost in aesthetics. A state-of-the-art hospital with only mediocre caregivers pales in comparison to a more modest facility with a friendly, capable staff.

Save your questions for your actual meeting, but if you worry you may forget something important between now and then, jot down the issues that concern you most and bring this list with you when you return. These may be the same as or different from the concerns of other owners. If your adopted dog has an ongoing medical issue, for instance, you may want to ask the vet what you can do to best manage the situation. Or perhaps your concerns involve something other than your dog's health. If your dog is shy or fearful, you may want to ask whether he will be able to see the same vet each time he visits the hospital. Doing so may help him feel more comfortable. Other factors that might be important to you include whether your vet provides dental care—a definite advantage if your older dog's teeth are in need of a professional cleaning.

Schedule your tour at a time your dog can accompany you; observing his reactions to the vet and other staff members can help you decide if this is the right place for you to bring him. If you get a bad feeling, or if your dog seems to react poorly to the veterinarian, continue your search. Many dogs dislike going to the vet, but you owe it to your own dog to find him someone

Bring your new dog to the vet within 48 hours of acquiring him to make sure he is healthy.

who makes this process easier rather than more difficult.

Once you have found a veterinarian whom both you and your adopted dog are comfortable with, make a point of stopping by from time to time when your dog isn't scheduled for an exam or any vaccinations. This will help him see that the veterinary hospital can be a fun place. You don't need to stay long. Just a quick greeting and a dog cookie from whomever is on duty should do the trick. Many hospitals keep a jar of treats right at the front counter for this very purpose.

WHEN YOU CAN'T BE HOME: EMPLOYING THE CARE OF OTHERS

Whether you work full time and need regular day care for your adopted dog or you take a single vacation a year, you will need someone to look after your dog when you cannot. If you have a responsible friend or family member with whom you feel comfortable leaving your dog when you're away, you might be all set. If that person has other pets or children who could pose a concern, though, you may want to contemplate using a boarding service or kennel instead. If it is ongoing day care you need, it might be too much to ask of a friend—even the most dependable.

Boarding Kennels

Be sure to tour a kennel before deciding if it is best for your dog. The most important factors are the cleanliness of the facilities, friendliness of the staff, and amount of time each day your dog will be taken out of his pen for exercise. A kennel will ask that you show proof of your dog's vaccinations—usually rabies, DHLP-P (distemper/parvo combination), and bordetella (kennel cough). Some also require an intestinal parasite test. These requirements ultimately protect your dog because all the others animals have been held to the same standard.

Doggy Day Care

Dog day care differs from boarding kennels in that you utilize a day care service five days a week, or however many days your schedule requires. Day care facilities also usually spend more time focusing on entertainment and exercise. Most programs offer both free and organized playtimes, along with walks and other physical activities. The caregiver you choose should use an assessment plan for deciding which dogs are compatible and therefore allowed supervised interaction. Issues of size, breed, and temperament should all be considered. Not all dogs are suitable candidates for day care; for the safety of all involved, some are turned away.

If you are away from home and can't take your dog with you, a qualified pet sitter or doggy day care facility may be the answer.

The benefits of placing your dog in day care are numerous. In addition to exercise and mental stimulation, he will receive the added benefit of socialization. Being around other dogs is excellent experience if you plan to add another dog to your household in the future. If not properly socialized, dogs can become very resistant to the idea of other canines in their households. Day care also offers your dog contact with other humans, which can be extremely helpful if your adopted dog suffers from separation anxiety.

In touring a day care facility, you should apply the same criteria used in evaluating a boarding service. You will need to show proof of the same vaccinations as for a kennel, but many day care facilities also require that your dog be spayed or neutered. Ask a lot of questions. Because your dog will be spending a significant amount of time in this setting, it is vital that you trust the staff.

Although prices can vary by region, the cost of day care may be higher than that of boarding facilities because more caregivers are needed—but like a children's day care, the most important matter is that you are leaving your dog in a healthy, safe environment. This is an expanding industry, so take time to find a day care that fits both your budget and comfort level.

Finding a Pet Sitter

The National Association of Professional Pet Sitters (NAPPS) is a nonprofit group that certifies and screens experienced pet sitters for knowledge and integrity. To find a member near you, visit www.petsitters.org or call them toll-free at 1-800-296-PETS.

Pet Sitters

If your adopted dog doesn't get along well with other dogs, don't despair. A professional pet sitter or dog walker may be the answer. A pet sitter will come to your home and stay with your dog for a predetermined amount of time while you're away. In many ways, this can be even better than day care because your dog will receive individual attention. A dog walker is similar to a pet sitter in that this experienced person will come to your home and take your dog for walks while you're away so that he can get out of the house and relieve himself when necessary. If your biggest concern is that you cannot make it home during the day to take your dog for his walk, this may be an ideal solution.

One of your best resources for referrals in this area is your veterinarian. Interview either a pet sitter or a dog walker thoroughly. Be sure to ask for references, and follow up by contacting them. You will trust this person with both your precious new pet and the keys to your home.

As the time nears to bring your new pet home, you may worry that you have overlooked something. Don't let this nagging feeling get in the way of enjoying your dog's homecoming. If he needs something specific that you haven't already gotten for him, you can always add it to your shopping list after his arrival. What matters most is that you are there to welcome him with open arms.

WELCOME
to the Family

Bringing an adopted pet home for the first time can be an exciting event for any new owner. Unfortunately, too much excitement can be overwhelming for many adopted dogs. Some careful planning, however, can help make your dog's homecoming a positive experience for everyone involved.

BRINGING YOUR ADOPTED DOG HOME

Plan your dog's arrival for a time when you can be home with him for the remainder of the day. Taking a few days or even a full week off from work to spend with him as he settles into his new home can be helpful if you can manage it, especially if housetraining is on the agenda. Avoid spending every moment with your dog, though, because you don't want him to have a hard time adjusting when it is time for you to return to your other responsibilities.

If possible, everyone in your household should be there to welcome your new dog, but it is best to let him approach each person on his own. Place a container of dog treats nearby so that family members can offer him one, but discourage them from calling his name at once or competing for his attention because this may confuse him. Once everyone has had a chance to say hello, attention should then be shifted away from your pet for a while.

If your adopted dog will be sharing his new home with another canine, it is wise to plan their first encounter outside the home. Ideally, you should bring both dogs to a park or another area a short distance from your home. Coming together in this neutral territory can make the resident dog feel less threatened by the new arrival, and it can make the meeting feel less intimidating to your newly adopted pet. Keep both dogs on leashes and allow them to move toward each other slowly, but don't push either one of them in the other's direction. They must get to know each other at their own pace.

Wait until the next day to introduce your new pet to your friends and neighbors. Let his first night be about getting acquainted with his new family and acclimating himself to his surroundings. Every dog responds differently to a new home. If he seems

Plan your new dog's homecoming for a time when you can be home with him for the remainder of the day.

interested in playing, grab one of his toys. If he nuzzles up to you while you're watching the news, rub his belly. But if he seeks out a quiet corner for a nap, just let him be.

Place your dog's bed (or crate, if that's where he'll be sleeping) either in or as close to your bedroom as possible. If you remand your dog to a faraway room of your home at night, he may feel scared, especially during his first night in an unfamiliar setting. This could lead to fussing or howling, and a sleepless night for everyone.

Many dog trainers advise against allowing dogs to sleep on their owners' beds. While keeping a dog off the bed is indeed a smart and effective strategy for enforcing the human–canine hierarchy, I never recommend banishing a dog from your bed unless he shows signs of aggression. If your dog is friendly, and you don't mind sharing your bed with someone who may snore, I say go for it. These days, even down comforters are machine washable.

Whatever your house rules—no begging at the table or chasing the cat, for example—now is the time to start enforcing them. If you don't want your dog sleeping on your bed, making an exception the first night will only make it harder for you to say no later and harder for your dog to have to move to another spot then. If you only want your dog to eat healthy foods, as you should, make sure every household member understands that this means no sharing junk food with him. By adhering to your own rules, you make it easier for your adopted dog to accept and follow them. Even a dog who was abused by a previous owner needs rules and structure in his life, perhaps even more so than other pets because there is comfort in predictability.

SETTING UP A SCHEDULE

Schedules give dogs a sense of permanence and routine. Although it might be tempting to wait a while before beginning big jobs like housetraining, postponing this and other important training tasks will only make them more difficult for your pet later on. As soon as you get home with your dog, show him right to his potty spot to give him an opportunity to relieve himself. This will help him understand right from the beginning that this is where he will be eliminating.

Even if you're on vacation from work, the first few days at home should mimic your typical routine as closely as possible. Instead of sleeping in, for example, start your day at your usual time. If you normally go for a morning run, lace up your sneakers and head out the door. If you want your dog to accompany you on your jogs, though, you may have to slow down your pace a bit while he gradually gets up to speed. If your kids' friends usually come over after school, tell them to make themselves at

Patience, Please

After doing your homework and searching for just the right dog for you, you probably can hardly wait to bring your adopted dog home and get started on your new life together. So you may be a little surprised or hurt if your new pet seems less than enthused when he finally walks through the door. Even if your dog warmed up to you quickly at the shelter or when you met him with the rescue volunteers, he may react to his homecoming with a certain amount of trepidation. Try not to take this personally or worry too much. Remember, your dog has spent the last few days or weeks in the unfamiliar environment of the shelter or a foster home. Now he is being faced with having to acclimate to yet another new place. Also, try not to put too much pressure on him. If the entire family has gathered to celebrate your dog's arrival but your dog just wants to scope out a quiet corner, let him. He may be worried that, just like his last owner, you aren't in this for the long haul. He may need a little time before he understands that your home is now his forever home. In the meantime, give him lots of love and plenty of patience.

home—after introducing everyone to your new dog, of course. The best way to help your dog settle into your family's routine is by living as you normally would and including your new pet in your activities whenever possible.

For owners who have never lived on a schedule themselves, a routine may be a bit of a change. Rest assured that a routine doesn't have to be boring. Make exercise and playtime key parts of your dog's day. If it's summer time, take him to the beach for a run. If it's snowing, go outside together to make snow angels. Groom him out on your deck, or garnish his dog food at meal time with parsley and carrots, yummy treats that are also good for him. What's important is that he can depend on you to be there with him when it's time to eat, to play, or to be taken outside to his potty spot. When you can't be there, you must make sure someone else is so that your dog's schedule isn't affected by a change in yours.

FORGING RELATIONSHIPS

Owners must understand that bonding is a process. Under the best circumstances, it can take time for an adopted dog to trust his new owners. Even eight-week-old puppies don't bond with their new owners overnight. As your dog settles into his new surroundings and gets to know everyone, though, he gradually becomes more comfortable with both his new home and new family members. He sees for himself every day that you are there to feed him, play with him, and take care of all his other needs. It is out of all these things that your dog's trust in you develops and the bond between you and your adopted pet deepens.

Your Dog's Relationship With You

The most important thing you can do for your adopted dog is to spend time with him. Just as you have made tangible space in your life for your pet, you must also set aside a certain amount of time for meeting all your dog's needs. When you spend time brushing or bathing him, whether you realize it at that moment or not, you are strengthening the bond between you. Morning walks and afternoon play sessions are also great ways to spend time forging this important new relationship.

Spending time together doesn't always mean attending to your dog's needs, however. Your dog also must learn to adapt to your life. Be sure to spend a certain amount of time each day going about your own daily business. Wash the dishes and do the laundry, entertain guests, and read that mystery novel for your next book club meeting.

My own dogs accompany me to my laundry room each and every time I go there to sort the clothes or empty the dryer. I joke that all the trips they make up and down the stairs of my home are the reason they are in such good shape. Damon loves curling up with me on the couch whenever I read in the evenings. Molly, who isn't much of a cuddler herself, will predictably grab one of her favorite chew toys at these times and lie on her back while chewing them, basking in the moment, too. Their favorite time of day is when everybody's home and in one room together. They care very little about what each of us is actually doing.

The most important thing you can do for your adopted dog is to spend time with him.

Don't feel guilty when you must go out to run errands or you want to go out to dinner with someone. Time apart, in reasonable quantities, is good for your relationship with your pet, too. Nothing shows how much your dog has missed you better than the excited greeting he will give you when you return home.

Make sure your dog spends time with other family members, too. Even if your adopted pet is primarily your responsibility, it is important for him to form a positive relationship with each person residing in your home. In addition to making household life more fun, this also makes it easier when you cannot be there to care for your pet. Your dog may bond most closely to you, but he should be comfortable spending time with every family member.

If you usually work late on Thursdays, this could be a wonderful time for your

Help your children to bond with your new adopted dog by teaching them how to interact with him appropriately.

husband to take your kids and the dog to the park each week. If your daughter is driving to the video store to drop off a DVD, ask her to invite your dog along for the ride. Also, involve the whole family in caring for your pet. Delegate certain tasks to various family members, making sure each job is age appropriate. You mustn't send your seven-year-old son outside to walk your 120-pound (54 kg) Bull Mastiff by himself, but he can be in charge of attaching his leash whenever you take him for a walk together—and giving him a treat when he heels on command.

Your Dog's Relationships With Children

The most important step in helping your children bond with your adopted dog is making safety your top priority. Encourage your kids to spend time with your new pet, but make sure you are always there to supervise. Never let a young child chase or pester your dog. Explain to your kids that they must respect your dog's wishes if he wants to move away from them. Because children sometimes have a tendency to play roughly, young family members also must understand that horseplay of any kind is not allowed with your new pet. Involving your children in your dog's training will help to show him that he must respect and treat them gently as well.

Encourage your kids to play with your dog. When they get home from school, when they tell you they're bored, when you are making dinner—these are all ideal times for an energetic play session. Kids can help your dog get the exercise he needs while also getting their own. If you have a fenced backyard, stand by the window while you do the dishes or sit and drink a cup of tea outside while you watch your kids and dog wear each other out.

I often joke that I wish I had my nine-year-old son Alec's energy. He gets up a half hour early each day just to take our two dogs for a walk with me. At first this was my idea: to strengthen his bond with them, to increase his level of responsibility, and to give us all a little extra exercise. Soon, however, Alec began rising before I did and reminding me that, even on rainy days, this was an important task. One of the most rewarding things about having kids and animals is how much we end up learning from them both.

Many families have found another wonderful way for their children and adopted dogs to bond: over a good book. Whether your child is a prolific bookworm or a struggling reader, having your child read aloud to your dog can be a smart way for her to forge a bond with your new pet. Reading is a quiet activity your child and her new canine friend can share. Many dogs delight in sitting alongside kids as they read, and the feeling is often mutual. Even children who normally shy away from reading out loud in school usually find dogs to be ideal reading partners. Unlike teachers and classmates—and

Always Supervise Kids and Dogs

One point that I cannot stress enough is the importance of always supervising the interactions between dogs and children. No matter how friendly or well trained a dog is, he may bite if provoked. Both kids and dogs must be taught how to treat each other properly, but neither can be trusted to follow these instructions faithfully when no adult is in the room. Children can get extremely excited in the presence of pets, and many dogs will act instinctively if they feel their safety is threatened. Even once your adopted dog has shown himself to be friendly around kids, you must remain vigilant. It only takes a moment for a dangerous bite to occur. If you must leave the room for just a moment to answer the door or telephone, take your younger children with you. If your older son or daughter wants to take your dog for a walk, accompany them. Also, just being in the same room doesn't necessarily mean being present. A dangerous bite can occur right behind your back while you are answering an e-mail. For the sake of all involved, supervise your dogs and kids whenever they are together—both for their safety and your own peace of mind.

even parents—dogs don't care when kids make mistakes. Dogs don't correct mispronunciations, and they don't laugh when a child stumbles over a word, like their friends might. Dogs don't even care if they hear the same story over and over.

Your Dog's Relationships With Other Pets

If yours is a multi-pet household, relationships between your adopted dog and your other animals (perhaps more than any other) can take time to form. In some cases, your dog may never become as close as you'd like with your beloved Siamese cat. Sometimes animals of opposite sex get along better than same-sex pets, but even this is not guaranteed.

The best way to help your adopted dog forge positive relationships with the other animals in your home is to give them a little space and a whole lot of time. Interactions between pets should always be supervised, but this doesn't mean that owners should interfere when minor squabbles erupt. It is usually better to let the animals work disagreements out themselves, providing neither party is being hurt.

In every relationship, one animal will be dominant over the other. This is the way of the animal world. By allowing your pets to work out this natural hierarchy on their own, you help maintain peace in your household. Usually, it is the resident pet that will take the dominant role. In other situations, however, the adopted dog has a more assertive temperament. You may find it difficult to understand why your 60-pound (27-kg) Lab begins submitting to your 6-pound (3-kg) Chihuahua-Poodle mix, but trying to intercede will only make the situation worse.

As soon as your pets have decided who the top dog will be (and this part rarely takes long), you can make household interactions easier on everyone by respecting the situation as it stands. If your resident dog has maintained his place of authority in the canine pack order, discourage your new pet from challenging this by respecting the resident dog's position. Make a habit of taking the resident dog for his walks first,

feed him before your adopted dog, and hand out treats and new toys in the same order. As long as everyone is getting the same amount of attention and everything else they need, no one is missing out on a thing.

Introduce your new dog to resident pets gradually to allow them time to get to know one another.

Relationships between different species sometimes just aren't possible. If you have decided to adopt a Jack Russell Terrier, for example, and your daughter has a pet gerbil, interactions between the two pets will not be possible. In fact, the only safe way to allow these specific animals to cohabitate is with a securely closed door—and I wouldn't put it past the Jack Russell to figure out how to open it.

CARING FOR YOUR ADOPTED DOG

Caring for an adopted dog involves many tasks and even more decisions. What type of food should you feed your adopted dog? How often will he need grooming? Will you need to hire a professional dog groomer? Which medical problems can you treat on your own at home, and which will demand that you bring your new pet to the vet? The answers to these questions will depend somewhat on your individual dog as well as on your own comfort level with particular tasks.

Feeding

Initially, your adopted dog should continue eating whatever food his previous owner fed him. If this is a quality kibble, it may be best to continue on the same regimen for the foreseeable future. If, however, your dog has been eating a nutritionally inferior food, gradually transition him to a higher-quality diet as soon as he seems to have adjusted to his new home. For some dogs, this may be the second week; for others it may be the second month. Because a dog's diet can have such a dramatic effect on both his health and temperament, though, don't wait any longer than this. Depending on your dog's individual circumstances, your veterinarian or trainer may suggest making a dietary change even sooner.

Selecting the Appropriate Food

You will pay a little more for a premium dog food, but in most cases this is money well spent. Low-priced foods, like those sold at grocery stores, usually contain large amounts of filler ingredients. They may include animal by-products and inexpensive protein sources like bone meal. By-products are parts of an animal not considered fit for human consumption such as hooves, beaks, and feet.

Inferior food brands also use chemical preservatives such as butylated hydroxyanisole (BHA), butylated hydroxytoluene (BHT), and ethoxyquin. Although the US Food and Drug Administration (FDA) currently allows pet food manufacturers to use a small amount of these preservatives in their foods (0.02 percent of the fat content only), all three preservatives have come under particular scrutiny in recent years. The FDA has even made a special point of asking manufacturers to lower the levels of ethoxyquin in their foods, but this preservative is still allowed in dog foods at levels of up to 150 parts per million (ppm) or 0.015 percent.

Quality foods contain human-grade meats and meat meal. Many of these foods are made from lean meats like lamb, venison, and herring. You can also find healthy foods made from more typical dog food ingredients such as beef and chicken. Whatever meat your dog prefers, it should be the primary ingredient in the food you choose for him. To find this information, check the package label; by law, dog food ingredients must be listed there in descending order according to weight.

For prepackaged foods to remain fresh, they must contain a preservative of some sort. The healthiest foods are preserved with tocopherols, vitamin-based preservatives. The only known downside to these natural preservatives is a shorter shelf life, but most dogs have no problem finishing a bag of dry food before its expiration date.

If your adopted dog is a picky eater, consider feeding him canned food instead of dry kibble. Often the smell of wet food alone can entice a reluctant eater to come running to his bowl at dinner time. (If not, pop a plate of wet food in the microwave for a few seconds. Heat will intensify the smell.) Canned foods are smart choices for older dogs with missing or decaying teeth. Most companies make both dry and canned foods, but the wet varieties make it necessary for owners to brush their dogs' teeth more frequently; moist foods tend to morph into calculus (the technical term for tartar) much faster than kibble.

Other common feeding alternatives include homecooked and raw diets. Homecooking has evolved into an incredibly common practice among pet owners. By hand-selecting the foods your dog eats, you help to ensure that he is consuming the healthiest diet possible. Because most of these foods are fresh, there is no need for preservatives at all. You must be certain with this feeding method, however, that your dog is getting a sufficient amount of all the nutrients he

Your dog's daily diet should contain the proper amount of proteins, vitamins, minerals, and other essential nutrients.

needs, otherwise a prepackaged brand may in fact be healthier.

Raw food regimens, commonly called BARF (short for "bones and raw food") diets, offer foods that most closely match the natural diet of wild dogs. Owners can choose to prepare raw foods at home for their pets, or they may purchase prepackaged frozen meals. Proponents of raw feeding regimens, which contain both meats and vegetables, maintain that this is the way dogs were meant to eat. They also assert that their dogs' health is strong evidence of the benefits of this type of feeding plan. Clean teeth and shiny coats are definite perks to raw feeding, but disadvantages also exist. Although the canine species is known for having a near cast-iron stomach, bacteria like *E. coli* and *salmonella* can make your dog sick. Even freezing the meat does not necessarily eliminate the presence of these microorganisms. Also, if a bone becomes caught in your dog's throat or lodged in his intestines, this can be fatal.

The Importance of Water

One of the most undervalued nutrients for both animals and humans is water. Just a 10-percent loss of your dog's total body water can lead to serious illness; a loss of 15 percent or more will cause death. Water is the primary vehicle for transporting nutrients throughout your dog's body and for removing wastes from his system in the form of urine. It helps with digestion and circulation and is also responsible for regulating body temperature. Moreover, whatever amount of water your dog loses throughout the day, he needs to consume an equal amount for replacement. Fresh water must always be available to your dog—not only at mealtime, but at all other times as well.

Feeding More Than One Dog

If you have more than one dog, feed them separately. Not only does this help to prevent arguments over food, but it also helps you make sure that each dog is eating his own food. Some dogs are gluttonous when it comes to eating and are certainly not above helping themselves to their housemates' food bowls. In other situations, one dog may be on a different type of diet altogether

due to an allergy or illness. In any of these instances, you want
to know that each dog is getting the food he needs to be healthy.

Special Diets

If your dog has medical problems, a prescription diet may be
necessary. These prepackaged foods are specially formulated to
meet the needs of dogs with specific illnesses and other
conditions. Dogs suffering from kidney disease, for example,
require diets low in both protein and phosphorus. Those
suffering from food allergies may be placed on hypoallergenic
regimens for a fixed period of time before adding new
ingredients back into their diets, one at a time. Prescription diets
are sold exclusively at veterinarian's offices, and like
prescription medications, they require a vet's authorization.

Free Feeding Versus Scheduled Feeding

Free feeding, or leaving food available to your dog at all
times, can be problematic at any age, but this is especially true
for dogs at either end of the age spectrum. Owners must be

If Your Dog Won't Eat

Sometimes the stress of losing a home, entering a shelter or breed rescue, and being placed with a new family can have an ill effect on a dog's appetite. If your adopted dog doesn't seem to be interested in eating, and the problem lasts for more than a day or two, schedule an appointment with his veterinarian. First, the vet will want to examine your pet to rule out an underlying physical condition that may be contributing to the problem. If he is healthy, the next step will be discussing your feeding options. Sometimes just taking the time to hand-feed your dog can make a difference. (This is also a great exercise for building trust!) If this doesn't work, try swapping kibble with canned food and warming it up to entice your reluctant eater. You can also moisten dry food with water before heating it for a similar effect.

In some cases, homecooking may be necessary. Few dogs can resist a homecooked meal of chicken and rice. If your ultimate goal is for your dog to return to eating kibble, though, try mixing his prepackaged food with homecooked fare. Once your dog begins eating again, you can then gradually decrease the amount of chicken and rice, replacing it with his dry food. Another option that often works well is topping dry food off with meat gravy or chicken broth. Praise your dog for eating even small amounts of food. As he settles into his new home, his appetite will likely return to normal.

As dog owners, we sometimes make situations more complicated than they need to be. I once read about an adopted Rottweiler who wouldn't eat if his new owners were watching him. Their solution? To place his bowl in front of him and then immediately leave the room. Whenever they returned, the food would be gone.

The best indication of whether your dog is getting enough food is his weight. Check this number regularly to make sure he isn't losing (or gaining) too much. Your vet can help you determine your dog's ideal weight range.

certain that their younger dogs are getting adequate nutrition for proper growth. This can be difficult to do when they aren't certain when or how much their dogs are eating. A more erratic feeding plan like this can also make housetraining significantly more challenging. An older dog faces an increased risk of many illnesses, so being aware of any changes in his appetite can help alert you to a problem before it intensifies. This too can be tricky for the owner of a free-fed dog.

An adult dog may do fine on a free-feeding plan, but bear in mind that changing back to a schedule takes far more time and effort than switching from a routine to free feeding. If the plan you have chosen is working for you and your dog, there should be no reason to make a change. If you find yourself in the midst of trying to bring the routine back, though, be patient. Divide the amount of food your dog is eating each day into several equal portions so that servings may be offered at various times.

If your adopted dog refuses to eat, resist the temptation to leave his bowl out until his appetite returns; an average meal should last only about 10 minutes. You must be consistent in offering food again at the next interval, however, to prevent your dog's blood sugar from dropping. Small dogs are sometimes susceptible to hypoglycemia (the technical name for this problem), and going long periods of time without food only heightens this risk.

Whether large or small, your adopted dog may need to eat a little more during the winter when the weather turns colder. Likewise, a dog's appetite can wane a bit when summertime temperatures soar. If this happens, don't panic, but do make sure he is eating at least some food at each meal. Provide him with plenty of cool water to keep him hydrated, and avoid taking him outside during the hottest times of the day. If your dog stops eating entirely, contact your veterinarian immediately because this is a sign of serious illness.

Grooming

Grooming your dog regularly is important for several reasons. First and foremost, tasks like brushing and bathing keep your adopted dog looking and feeling good. Good grooming is also a smart step toward keeping your dog healthy. When you brush your dog, check his fur for any abnormalities: fleas or ticks, dry spots, or lumps or bumps. These changes can signal a variety of health problems. In addition to these more practical reasons for grooming, keeping your dog neat and clean also can be fun. Many dogs love the one-on-one attention from their owners that grooming provides.

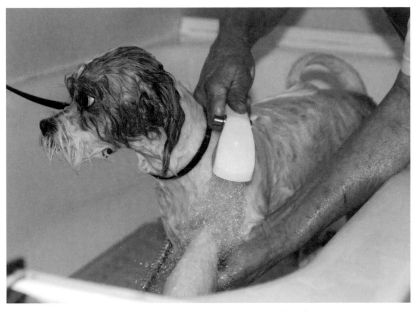

Regular grooming keeps your dog looking and feeling good and helps to ensure his overall health.

Brushing and Combing Your Dog

If your dog has long hair, daily brushings are best for him, especially if his hair is fine and prone to snarling. Shorter coats can go a few days to a week between brushings, but don't put this important task off any longer than this. Besides preventing tangles from forming, brushing also removes dead hair and dirt from your dog's coat. This lessens shedding—a problem for a surprising number of short-haired breeds—and also can make bathing necessary less often.

Always brush your dog completely before bathing him. Once wet, any mats that he does have will be considerably harder to remove from his fur. To make sure you've done a proper job, comb his hair after you finish brushing.

How to Bathe Your Dog

Many owners worry that frequent bathing will dry out a dog's coat and skin. The truth is that insufficient rinsing is responsible for this problem. You can bathe your dog as often as you like—as frequently as once a week, if necessary—provided that you use a quality shampoo made specifically for dogs and remove all of this cleanser from the coat each time you use it.

Using a shampoo and conditioner designed for your dog's hair type keeps his coat in proper shape. If you prefer to lengthen the time between your dog's baths as much as possible, brush him as often as you can.

If your dog is small enough, the kitchen sink may serve as an acceptable bathtub, but be sure to use a skid-proof mat and never leave your pet unattended. A fall from this height could be catastrophic for a tiny dog. Larger dogs can be bathed right in the bathtub. Again, take safety precautions like using a mat to prevent slipping. Regardless of where you bathe your dog, gather all your supplies, including towels, shampoo, and even your telephone, before running the water. If you run to answer a call once your dog has jumped in, he will most certainly jump back out as soon as he's left alone. Also, remember to take your dog for a pre-bath potty break, and turn up the thermostat during colder times of the year before placing him in the tub. Just like people, dogs feel chilled when they first get out of a bath.

You may dry your dog's fur with a blow dryer or let him air dry on his own as long as the temperature inside your home is warm enough. If you're using a dryer, avoid the hottest setting because it can burn his skin. If your dog has long hair, brush him repeatedly during drying to prevent any knots from forming. Regardless of the weather, avoid taking him outdoors until he is thoroughly dried. Recently washed dogs have an uncanny knack for finding—and rolling in—dirt, especially while still wet.

Nail and Dental Care

It's not just your dog's hair that needs grooming. His nails and teeth must also receive regular attention. Clip his nails about once or twice a month, depending on how quickly they grow. If you can hear your dog's nails when he walks across the floor, they are already overdue for a trim. Overgrown nails can be painful for your pet to walk on, and they can be caught on clothing or carpeting. If your dog eats wet food, brush his teeth daily. If he eats kibble, you must still perform this important task as frequently as possible. By keeping your dog's teeth clean, you keep his mouth healthy and his breath fresh. Chew toys like the ones Nylabone makes also help to prevent plaque and tartar buildup.

Inspect your dog's teeth, eyes, and ears weekly.

Eye and Ear Care

Your dog's eyes and ears also need regular cleaning. Many light-colored dogs are prone to tear staining, but all dogs should have their eyes wiped from time to time to prevent infection. Use a soft, damp cloth to wipe each eye gently about once a week, more often for dogs who produce a greater amount of eye discharge. If left to harden, debris in this sensitive area can be more difficult to remove later.

Long ears should be cleaned about once a week. Squirt a small amount of ear cleanser onto a cotton ball and gently wipe the ear flap. Never use cotton swabs inside the ear because they can injure your pet. A little bit of wax is healthy for the canine ear, but too much dirt and bacteria can lead to dangerous and painful infections. Short- or prick-eared dogs aren't as prone to infections because their ears naturally receive better air flow, but these dogs also should have their ears cleaned at least once or twice a month.

Professional Grooming Services

You may wonder if you should groom your adopted dog yourself or hire a professional for some or all of these jobs. If you feel comfortable with the idea and would like to save a bunch of money, I highly recommend grooming your dog personally. Although it can take some time to learn all the ins

Easing Your Pet's Grooming Fears

It's important that your pet tolerate being groomed by you, regardless of how often you take him to a professional. To train your pet to accept being handled in this way, groom him briefly when you're both relaxed. For example, begin by gently massaging his coat each morning as you feed him. Gradually introduce a brush or comb. Each day, increase grooming time and work on different areas of his body. Reward your pet for cooperating. The more comfortable he feels being handled by you and pet by strangers, the better he'll tolerate professional grooming.

(Courtesy of the Humane Society of the United States)

and outs of grooming, you don't have to produce professional results. You also can combine forces with a family member or friend to make grooming a bit easier for both you and your dog. If you don't have time for grooming, though, it is far better to hire a professional than to postpone these necessary tasks. I also recommend using a groomer for cutting nails if you've had too many mishaps.

You mustn't expect a groomer to undo weeks or months of neglect, however. Some tasks, like brushing, must be done at home regularly to keep your dog in proper shape. If you are too frightened to trim your dog's nails on your own, ask your pet supply store if it offers this service for their patrons. Many do for a nominal fee. For many owners, this is an efficient means of keeping their dogs' feet in proper condition between trips to the groomer.

Selecting a Professional Groomer: If you decide to utilize the services of a professional, you must find a groomer who will fulfill your grooming needs while treating your dog with the same amount of care and respect as you do. It is of the utmost importance that you trust not only this person's abilities, but also his or her genuine fondness for animals. More than anything else, listen to your instincts. Choosing a groomer is a lot like selecting a day care provider. You will, after all, be leaving your precious pet in this person's charge for the better part of a day each time he needs to be groomed. You will want to ask many questions and carefully inspect the facilities before making your decision.

Getting Referrals: Although you can easily find a dog groomer by simply thumbing through your local phonebook, a better place to start is by getting referrals from your breeder, veterinarian, or a friend who uses a groomer's services. Recommendations from these trusted individuals are invaluable, and they prevent you from having to start your search based on such superficial information as which business has the best ad. Another good resource for new dog owners seeking a groomer is checking the National Dog Groomers Association of America website at www.nationaldoggroomers.com.

Bear in mind that no government agency regulates or licenses pet groomers. Although many are registered or certified by their individual training schools or other organizations, it is still extremely important to interview a potential groomer and tour the facilities before leaving your dog there.

Initial questions may pertain to costs, hours of operation, and other general policies. If you think the business may be able to meet your needs, ask for references and follow up by contacting them. You should also contact your local Better Business Bureau to find out if any complaints have been filed against the company.

Even if you don't plan to depend on someone else for grooming, it may be a wise idea to utilize this kind of service at least occasionally. Helping your dog become more comfortable in the hands of others can only have a positive effect on his temperament. At the very least, it may be an excellent exercise in socialization that offers you a pleasant break in the process.

If you'd rather not groom your dog yourself, seek the services of a professional groomer.

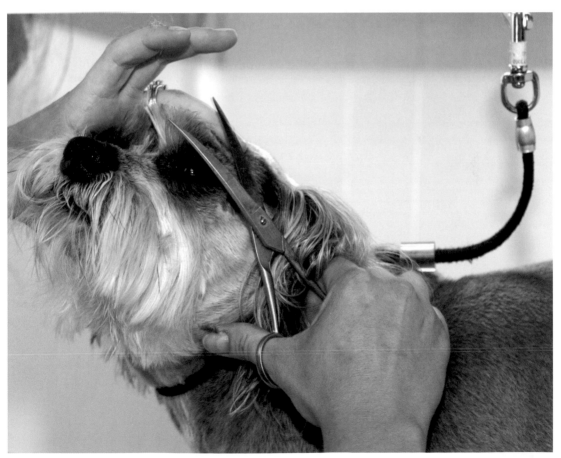

Health

Keeping your adopted dog healthy begins with taking him to see his veterinarian regularly, but it doesn't end there. Your vet can help you stay on top of important issues like vaccinations, prevention and treatment of parasites, and monitoring for the most common illnesses that affect dogs of your pet's breed, size, or age. By familiarizing yourself with the afflictions that are most likely to strike your dog, you can help him avoid most of these problems. And when an illness does strike, you will be prepared to deal with it quickly and effectively.

Because shelter dogs are housed with so many other animals from a variety of different backgrounds and living conditions, schedule your adopted dog's first veterinary exam right away. Shelter dogs are exposed to a number of communicable diseases. While most facilities immunize their animals against the most dangerous of these afflictions, the very nature of shelter life makes it impossible for all the dogs to be protected against every disease before they may be exposed to it. Even after a dog has been vaccinated for a particular illness, his body doesn't build full immunity toward it for another few days.

Vaccinations

Whether you adopt a puppy, adult, or senior dog, his vaccination schedule will begin before he is transferred to your care. However, he may be due for boosters (repeated doses of vaccines that ensure effectiveness) after his homecoming. Bring all the paperwork you received from the shelter or animal rescue to your dog's first appointment so that your veterinarian knows what vaccines have already been administered. You also will need to decide if you wish for your dog to be vaccinated against any additional afflictions, such as kennel cough and Lyme disease.

Vaccinations have become a subject of increasing debate in recent years. Similar to parents who are electing to place their children on delayed vaccination schedules to minimize harmful side effects, pet owners are also weighing the risks associated with immunizations. If their dogs do not fall into a high-risk category for a specific disease, more and more people are opting not to vaccinate for that particular illness. Vets and owners alike are also erring on the side of caution when it comes to the frequency of vaccination and the number of shots a dog receives in a single vet visit. Overvaccinating has been linked to thyroid disease, liver and kidney disease, and even cancer.

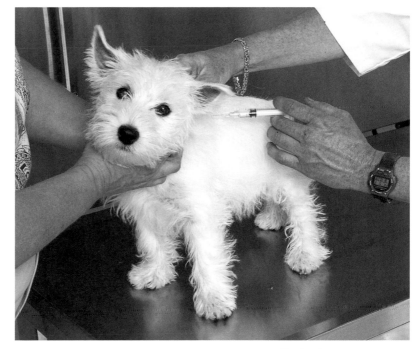

Vaccinations can prevent many life-threatening diseases from striking your pet.

Nevertheless, vaccinations can prevent many life-threatening diseases from striking your pet. Rabies, for example, is almost always fatal; the vaccination for this virus is also required by law in all 50 states in the United States. Because studies have shown that the rabies vaccination remains effective much longer than previously thought, many states are lengthening the time between necessary booster shots. What was once an annual vaccine is now required only every three years in these states. This same time table is currently typical for vaccinating against distemper and parvovirus as well.

So, which vaccines are necessary for your dog? The answers depend on several factors, including his age and overall health, the environment in which he lives, and the areas to which you take him on a regular basis. If you board your dog or take him to day care, for instance, the bordetella (kennel cough) vaccine may be a prerequisite for admission. If, however, your dog rarely visits public places frequented by other dogs, you may feel comfortable with skipping this shot because kennel cough is highly curable. Consult with your vet to make an informed decision.

If you find that making several different veterinary hospital appointments for vaccinations is too expensive, consider utilizing low-cost vaccination clinics. Many pet supply stores and animal organizations hold these popular events regularly. Just be sure to provide your regular veterinarian with copies of the paperwork you receive so that your dog's records remain current. You may also opt to administer some of your dog's vaccines yourself. By law, the rabies vaccine must be given by a licensed veterinarian, but other vaccines can be purchased from vet supply companies and administered at home. A third option is simply asking your veterinarian if he or she would consider waiving the additional office visit fees after your dog's initial exam. Many vets are more than willing to work with their clients, especially when it benefits the animals.

Sometimes the decision of whether or not to vaccinate for a specific illness is a tough one. Lyme disease, for example, is a serious affliction that can ultimately leave a dog unable to walk when left untreated. This might lead an owner to believe that vaccinating is the best choice. When Lyme disease is caught early, however, any permanent damage can be avoided through simple treatment with an antibiotic. If you live in Maine, as I do, vaccinating may still be the smarter option because 85 percent of Lyme disease cases are in the northeast and Wisconsin. If you live in California, on the other hand, you may be more moved by the fact that none of the 27 veterinary colleges in the United States recommend vaccinating for Lyme disease in areas where the incidence of Lyme disease is low.

Discuss vaccinations with your vet at your dog's first appointment, even if he isn't due for any shots. The best way to make a decision about these or any other health issues concerning your pet is by arming yourself with as much reliable information as possible and giving yourself the time to choose the best course of action for you and your pet. What you decide this year may be entirely different from the choices you make down the road as even more is learned about the vaccinating process. And remember to always observe your dog carefully in the hours and days following the inoculations he receives. Any dog can experience an allergic reaction to an immunization.

Allergies

Allergies are relatively common in pets. Just like numerous people, many dogs suffer from food allergies. Also similar to the problem in humans, identifying canine allergens

can be rather time-consuming. Although allergy tests are available, often the most effective route is good old-fashioned trial and error. If your dog's tummy seems to be consistently upset by his food, begin removing as few ingredients at once as possible (ideally just one at a time) and watch for any physical reactions. If no improvement is noticed after several days, return that item to your dog's diet and remove another until you can isolate the problem-causing agent. Common canine food allergens are corn and wheat, but because every dog is different, the problem could be literally anything. The best way to avoid this painstaking identification process is to introduce new foods to your dog slowly and one at a time.

Other common canine allergies involve skin reactions. Regular grooming (especially brushing) can help prevent these issues. Bear in mind, however, that bathing too frequently (or without a shampoo created to help a particular problem) can often aggravate a skin irritation. If your dog experiences severe itching, redness, or a rash, schedule an appointment with his veterinarian to determine the cause. Make note of when the problem first appeared and any other symptoms your dog also may have because this information may help the vet to diagnose the problem.

Fleas

Some of the most preventable canine illnesses are those caused by internal and external parasites. Fleas can attack dogs virtually anytime and anywhere, subjecting your pet to considerably more than a little bit of itching. For every flea you find on your dog, there will be plenty more developing in your home. Most dogs are allergic to the flea saliva that is left on an animal's skin once biting begins; some will scratch to the point of creating sores and skin infection. If left untreated, fleas can cause serious illness, including anemia and the transmission of tapeworms. In the case of severe infestation on a younger or debilitated dog, death can result. Even if your adopted dog is primarily an indoor pet, he is still at risk of infestation if not treated with a regular preventive.

The family cat can carry in enough fleas to make your dog equally miserable. Fleas thrive in warm temperatures, so your home is the perfect place for them to set up house; they can easily hide in such places as carpets, furniture, and even draperies. It doesn't matter if yours is the cleanest house on the block; fleas don't discriminate. They will feed off any host they can find—your dog, your cat, and even human family members.

Capable of jumping 13 inches (6 cm) or more horizontally, fleas can be difficult to locate and catch, but constant itching is the most reliable sign of their presence. They also tend to favor certain areas on dogs, including near the ears, on the neck and abdomen, and around the base of the tail.

An easy way to do a flea check on your dog is to use a flea comb. Gently run the comb through your dog's coat and then shake any matter left on the comb onto a moistened piece of white paper or tissue. If this foreign matter begins to dissolve, leaving a red stain, your dog probably has fleas. (The red color is caused by ingested blood in the fleas' feces.)

Preventive treatments recommended by your veterinarian are the safest and most effective route for combating fleas. Administered once a month, the majority of these topical solutions are applied to a small area of the dog's skin. The solutions then spread progressively over the body surface, ridding your dog of his current fleas within hours and also preventing future infestation. These medications must be used as prescribed by your vet, who will provide you with detailed

Besides intense itching, fleas can cause skin irritation and discomfort.

instructions on application after deciding on an appropriate dosage for your dog based on his weight.

If your dog has fleas, see your veterinarian as soon as possible. Also, remember to treat the environment as well as your dog. Flea bombs, also called foggers, can help rid your home of this nuisance, but check with your veterinarian before deciding on a plan of attack. (If your dog spends time outdoors, also ask about treating your yard.) Because you are dealing with highly toxic chemicals, carefully read labels and follow directions thoroughly. Most importantly, remember to remove all people and pets from the home before treating it. If your home is carpeted, make sure to vacuum thoroughly after a flea infestation and dispose of the bag immediately whether it is full or not.

Check with your veterinarian before using any over-the-counter flea or tick product. Organophosphate insecticides (OPs) and carbamates are found in various products and should be avoided because they pose particular health threats to children and pets, even when used correctly. A product contains an OP if the ingredient list contains chlorpyrifos, dichlorvos, phosmet, naled, tetrachlorvinphos, diazinon, or malathion. The product contains a carbamate if the ingredient list includes carbaryl or propoxur.

Ticks

If your dog spends any time outdoors, you will need to check him regularly for ticks. Ticks can easily crawl onto your pet and hold on for dear life, putting your dog at risk for serious disease. When a tick first attaches itself to your dog's skin, it may be difficult to spot due to its minute size and typical brownish-white coloring. But once it swells with blood, an engorged tick may reach the size of a plump pea. This may still be hard to see on both long- and short-haired dogs, so you must always be on the lookout. Ticks are most prevalent in the warmer months, but they can survive in temperatures as low as 35°F (2°C). Combing your dog whenever he has been outdoors is an excellent way to find anything that might be hiding within his coat before it can cause a serious problem.

The deer tick, also known as the black-legged tick, is especially difficult to notice because it is only the size of a sesame seed before becoming engorged with blood. Once it has fed, it will still only measure between 3 and 6 mm. This tick gets

Check your dog for ticks after he's been outdoors.

the most media attention in the United States because it is the best-known carrier of Lyme disease. Although not contagious, Lyme disease (named for the town in Connecticut where the first outbreak occurred) is a very serious illness for both dogs and people.

One of the most common signs of canine Lyme disease is limping, frequently with one of the front legs. Other signs include lymph node swelling in the affected limb and a fever. If left untreated, the disease will progress quickly, leaving the animal virtually unable to walk within just days. Treatment with an antibiotic is imperative. When caught early, permanent joint or nerve damage may be avoided. The best way to avoid the onset of Lyme disease is by having your dog vaccinated, but you will still need to check your dog regularly because many other types of ticks may be lurking in your own backyard.

If you find a tick on your dog, use a pair of tweezers to carefully remove it. It is vital that you get both the tick's head and body out, so your first objective will be getting the tick to simply let go on its own. To do this, use a pair of sterilized tweezers to grasp the tick's body and begin pulling it away from your dog's skin very gently. Apply steady pressure, but be sure not to squeeze too tightly. Jiggling the tick a bit is fine, but don't rotate it.

Some vets suggest using a drop or two of isopropyl alcohol to get a tick to release a stubborn grip, but according to the American Lyme Disease Foundation, this method can backfire, even increasing the chances of disease transmission. Once the tick is out, this is the time for the alcohol—drop the tick in some of this solution to kill it. Never use your bare hands or feet to kill a tick. As soon as the tick has been properly disposed of, clean the bite wound with disinfectant, and sterilize your tweezers with some fresh alcohol. If you cannot get the tick to release, or if you remove only part of it, seek assistance from your veterinarian.

Rocky Mountain spotted fever, ehrlichiosis (a bacterial infection), and babesiosis (a blood disorder) are just a few of the other dangerous illnesses ticks can transmit. Although there is no universal vaccine to prevent all the diseases caused by ticks, treating your dog with a regular preventive flea and tick medication can significantly reduce his risk of unwittingly playing host to these dangerous creatures. You will be protecting your human family from the many tick-transmitted illnesses that can endanger their health as well.

Heartworm

Mosquitoes are carriers of heartworm, a parasite that can cause your dog weeks of uncomfortable veterinary treatment and, in advanced cases, can take his life. Although many people erroneously believe that heartworm is only a threat to dogs in warm climates, the larval development of the mosquito species that serves as intermediate hosts for this disease can occur in temperatures as low as 57°F (14°C). Accordingly, many veterinarians have begun advising clients to use monthly heartworm preventives year round.

Your dog should be seen annually, preferably in early spring, for a blood test checking for heartworm disease. This test must be performed before your vet can provide you with heartworm preventive. Usually administered monthly, most preventives are available in the forms of either conventional pills or more palatable chewable versions that look and taste like treats. Consistency is especially important because these drugs can be 100 percent effective

Giving Your Dog Medication

Pills

1. With your dog sitting, gently open his mouth with one hand and drop the pill down the back of his throat with the other.

2. Hold your dog's mouth closed with his head pointed upward until he swallows and licks his lips, and then praise him extensively.

Tip: If your dog is especially resistant to taking pills, you may try hiding the pill in a small piece of meat, bread, or cheese. You may even buy special treats made with hollow centers for this purpose. Check with your vet first, though, because some medications should not be given with certain foods.

Liquids

1. Using a liquid syringe, expel the medication into the side of your dog's mouth.

2. Hold your dog's mouth closed immediately afterward until the medication is swallowed.

Tip: Occasionally offer your dog a liquid treat (such as a small amount of melted ice cream) from the syringe when he is healthy. This will help encourage him to readily take medication administered this way when he is sick.

Injections

1. After preparing the syringe, lift the fold of skin on the scruff of your dog's neck.

2. Insert the needle sideways into the skin, being careful not to come out the other side. Empty the syringe. This approach will help you avoid hitting muscle.

Note: Injections should only be administered at home at the instruction of your dog's veterinarian.

when given on the same day each month.

If your dog tests positive for heartworm, treatment must be started at once. Symptoms of heartworm disease include coughing, exercise intolerance, and abnormal lung sounds; however, a blood test is often the very first indicator. Treating the disease can be an extremely complicated and expensive procedure, with serious side effects. When caught early, successful treatment of this devastating illness is possible, although prevention is highly preferred.

Other Worms

Other parasites that may infest your dog are commonly referred to as worms. Thirty-four percent of dogs in the United States are infected with some kind of gastrointestinal parasite. This is why many shelters and rescues have all their dogs dewormed whether they show signs of being infested or not. Because the problem can return, however, you must always be on the lookout and bring stool samples to your vet regularly. Although the presence of certain types (such as roundworms and tapeworms) can easily be seen in your dog's stool, diagnosing others (such as whipworms and hookworms) can be more difficult. Signs of worms include excessive licking of the anal region or dragging the rear end.

Several of these parasites can also infest humans, so it is especially important to prevent them from attacking your dog in the first place. Keep your yard free of canine feces because soil contamination from excrement creates ideal conditions for many of these worms.

Never give your dog a dewormer (medication intended to rid a dog's body of worms) without the prior approval of and instructions from your vet. If your dog does become infested with worms, seek treatment at once (don't forget to bring that stool sample) and be sure to follow up by treating his environment to prevent further infestation.

Ear Problems

Whether your adopted dog suffers from an isolated ear infection or numerous recurrences of this problem, an ear infection can cause serious damage when overlooked. Typically, a dog suffering from an ear problem will tilt his head to one side, scratch at the ear, or shake his head from discomfort. The ear will often look red inside and may also have an unpleasant odor. If you suspect that your dog has an ear infection, schedule an appointment with his veterinarian right away because it won't go away without treatment with an antibiotic.

Mites, tiny crab-like parasites, can infest a dog's ear, causing symptoms amazingly similar to those of an ear infection. They are also highly contagious to other dogs and cats within the household.

If mites are present, your dog may have a thick, crusty, black ear discharge. It is likely that you won't be able to discern an ear infection from a mite infestation, though, without the help of your veterinarian, who will be able to easily identify either problem and prescribe the appropriate antibiotic or insecticide needed for treatment.

Eye Problems

As dogs age, they become more prone to a variety of problems related to their eyes. Even young dogs can develop these problems if eye issues run in their families. Many ocular conditions are treatable, some are not, but none are as scary as they may seem at first.

Cataracts: Although common, cataracts are fortunately painless and also highly treatable. The word cataract literally means "to break down"; in the case of this ophthalmologic condition, it is the transparency of the eye's lens that essentially breaks down, leaving an opaque film over the lens of the dog's eye. This film (or cataract), which interrupts the dog's vision, is usually extremely noticeable to an observant owner. Cataracts may be inherited or caused by a traumatic injury to the eye. The latter type will only affect the eye that has been wounded. Although there is no way to prevent or reverse cataracts, they can be surgically removed and replaced with an acrylic lens by a veterinary ophthalmologist. This procedure offers an impressive success rate of 90 to 95 percent in otherwise healthy dogs. Interestingly, this statistic remains the same regardless of how long a dog has had the cataract.

A third cause of cataracts can be the onset of diabetes. In this unique situation, the progression of the cataracts may actually be decelerated with successful treatment of the diabetes.

Cherry Eye: Another condition that may be triggered by an eye injury is commonly referred to as cherry eye. This affliction, formally known as nictitans gland prolapse, affects a dog's third eyelid. If you did not realize that your dog even had a third eyelid, you are not alone. Many owners learn of this additional lower lid only when the tear gland behind it becomes red and inflamed, protruding from the corner of the dog's eye.

Cherry eye is usually not painful to the dog, but it can be quite alarming to an unsuspecting owner upon discovery. In mild cases, a veterinarian will prescribe a steroid to reduce the swelling, but positive results are often temporary. Because long-term steroid use is usually best avoided, surgery is frequently the best solution. If left untreated, the mass may become

infected due to prolonged exposure. Your dog may also scratch at the eye, compounding the problem.

As dogs age, they become more prone to a variety of eye conditions and diseases.

Surgery for cherry eye once included the removal of the tear gland, but fewer vets are taking this approach; eliminating the gland leaves a dog more vulnerable to keratoconjunctivitis sicca (KCS), or dry eye. KCS is a serious condition that can result in redness, mucus discharge, and corneal scarring and ulceration—and ultimately even permanent sight loss.

Glaucoma: You may often hear the word glaucoma mentioned together with cataracts, but these are in fact two very different diseases. Unlike cataracts, which technically don't require treatment unless the pet becomes blind, glaucoma is a very serious disease that demands immediate medical attention. Also, unlike cataracts, glaucoma can be very painful.

Caused by intraocular pressure (pressure within the dog's eyeball), glaucoma may present with redness, cloudiness, tearing, loss of vision, an enlarged eyeball, uncharacteristic aggressiveness, lethargy, or a loss of appetite. The disease is most often congenital, but in rare cases it can be caused by a coexisting condition—a luxating (floating) lens that blocks the natural fluid drainage of the dog's eye. Regardless of its cause, glaucoma can result in irreversible vision loss within mere hours if the pressure is not relieved.

Progressive Retinal Atrophy (PRA) and Progressive Retinal Degeneration (PRD): Unfortunately, not all diseases that cause canine blindness can be alleviated with early intervention or surgical procedures. Progressive retinal atrophy (PRA) and progressive retinal degeneration (PRD) are two inherited disorders that cause gradual but inevitable vision loss. This is caused by the deterioration or atrophy (shrinkage) of the retina. A dog with PRA or PRD will likely begin bumping into things only at night or in low-light situations, but will eventually show signs of increasing vision loss regardless of the time of day or light quality. Although PRA and PRD have further symptoms (including dilated pupils and hyperreflectivity, or shininess, to the back of the eye), these signs are rarely noticeable until the disease has already reached an advanced stage.

If every cloud indeed has a silver lining, for PRA and PRD it is the amount of time that an owner is given to help prepare for his or her dog's eventual sight loss. Although it is natural for an owner to feel overwhelmed at first by the prognosis of permanent blindness, it is important to realize that your dog will be impacted by this deficit far less than a human being in a similar situation. Blind dogs can live enormously satisfying lives. Although some additional training will be necessary, most sightless dogs acclimate to this change easily by simply doing what they have always done—relying on their other, more valued senses, particularly hearing and smell.

Hip Dysplasia

Larger breeds such as German Shepherds and Labrador Retrievers are especially prone to hip dysplasia, but any dog can suffer from hip problems. Although good breeders test for hip dysplasia, it can still occasionally appear in some dogs who have been cleared; there is no way to guarantee that a dog won't develop the condition. Literally a malformation of the ball and socket in the hip joint, hip dysplasia is an inherited defect that usually doesn't cause noticeable symptoms until a dog is between six to eight months old. Although the condition may be mild, moderate, or severe, the signs are usually the same,

Hip and joint problems can prohibit your dog from running and playing.

including lameness, stiffness, and limping. Symptoms may be intensified on cold, damp days. A dog suffering from hip dysplasia may also exhibit an understandable change in temperament.

As the dog continues, however reluctantly, to move through the pain, the problem may seem to dissipate, but more likely this is simply the result of scar tissue that forms from the stretching and tearing of the joint. Eventually, degenerative arthritis also sets in and compounds the problem when symptoms return.

Diagnosis is made through veterinary examination and X-rays. A veterinarian may recommend surgery in extreme cases, but medical treatment is also possible. This may include enforced rest periods during times of acute discomfort, mild analgesics (pain killers), and anti-inflammatory drugs. Although surgical treatment may seem like a risky endeavor, many dogs return to a full activity level even after having a full hip replacement.

Hypoglycemia

Small dogs face an elevated risk of hypoglycemia. The medical term for low blood sugar, hypoglycemia is essentially the opposite of diabetes. Most dogs outgrow the problem naturally before they are even old enough to leave their mothers, but in some cases the condition remains a continued threat to the dog's health. At times, it can even be brought on by stress.

Symptoms of hypoglycemia include poor coordination, weakness, and glassy eyes. If your dog exhibits these signs, the first thing you should do is feed him food with a high sugar content, such as corn syrup. If he is especially weak, you may have to put a small amount on your finger and rub it on his gums. Never try to force any food down your dog's throat because he could choke. Your dog should also be kept warm. If he readily accepts the treat and can sit on his own, you may want to offer him a small meal. Next, contact your dog's veterinarian. Even if the episode passes easily with the help of a sugary treat, it is still vital that your vet knows about the incident. She will likely ask you to bring your dog in for an exam at this time.

Hypoglycemia is a very serious but manageable disease. If left untreated, a hypoglycemic dog can experience seizures, lose consciousness, or even die. Once a dog is diagnosed, however, his owner can control the disease by feeding smaller, more frequent meals. It is especially important that a dog with this condition doesn't miss a meal, so make arrangements for someone else to feed your pet if you are ever unable to make it home in time. If you take your dog on regular walks, it may be a good idea to take along liquid glucose packets. These can be purchased at most pharmacies.

Your veterinarian can help you select a food high in protein, fat, and complex carbohydrates that will help your dog best utilize his nutrients. You will generally want to avoid feeding simple sugars, but you might need to adjust your dog's diet accordingly if his exercise level increases because more frequent or intense physical activity may justify an increased sugar intake. Talk to your vet about the right plan for your dog.

Autoimmune Diseases

Autoimmune diseases are unique in that they cause a dog's own immune system to turn on itself. In the case of autoimmune hemolytic anemia (AIHA), it is the dog's red blood cells that are attacked, robbing the body of their oxygen-carrying properties. Once destroyed, portions of these cells are then passed through the dog's body in the urine.

Sometimes the cause of AIHA can be identified, such as with AIHA secondary to systemic lupus erythematosus (SLE). More often, however, the source cannot be verified. In many of these cases, the cause is often theorized to be a bacterial infection, medication, or vaccination.

Although the disease is treatable, battling AIHA can be difficult. Steroids are usually the preferred treatment option, but if the condition does not improve with their use alone, blood transfusions and chemotherapy may also be necessary.

Symptoms of AIHA include discolored urine (from expelled blood), pale complexion, and fatigue. A dog with AIHA may also have jaundice, a condition that presents with a yellow discoloration of the eyes, nose, and skin. As blood is lost, the dog's body weakens rapidly, so early diagnosis is vital.

Autoimmune thyroiditis is similar to AIHA, but instead of targeting red blood cells, autoimmune thyroiditis causes a dog's immune system to attack its own T3 and T4 thyroid hormones. The condition also destroys thyroglobulin, a substance

Your Dog's First-Aid Kit

The following items should always be kept on hand in the event of a medical emergency:

- antibiotic ointment
- canine first-aid manual
- children's diphenhydramine (antihistamine)
- corn syrup
- cotton swabs
- emergency phone numbers (including poison control, emergency veterinarian, and your dog's regular vet)
- hydrogen peroxide
- instant ice pack
- ipecac syrup
- liquid bandages
- nonstick gauze pads, gauze, and tape
- oral syringe or eyedropper
- rectal thermometer
- saline solution
- scissors
- soap
- styptic powder or pencil
- tweezers
- any other item your veterinarian recommends keeping on hand

You may also want to assemble a portable emergency kit for your dog if you spend a lot of time hiking, camping, or traveling together. With either type of kit, remember to keep an eye on expiration dates and toss any products before they should no longer be used.

necessary for forming such hormones. The symptoms of autoimmune thyroiditis are very similar to those of hypothyroidism because it is the same system being compromised in both situations. Diagnosis and treatment are also similar, but in the case of autoimmune thyroiditis, thyroid antibodies will be found in the dog's blood when tested.

Cancer strikes many older pets, but various treatment options are available that can help manage or stop the disease.

Cancer

Cancer can be one of scariest of all canine diseases. It is important to note that when this diagnosis is made, though, the word "cancer" no longer has the bleak connotation it once did. The disease most frequently strikes dogs over the age of 10, but a dog of any age or breed can be stricken with cancer and, more importantly, can beat it.

One of the most common cancers in dogs, mast cell tumors, can be treated with great success. Spaying dogs often prevents mammary tumors, the most common kind of cancer in female dogs. Similarly, testicular cancer is prevented in males with neutering.

Always be on the lookout for any suspicious-looking lumps or bumps on your dog. Most will end up being benign, but you can literally save your dog's life by just giving him a quick once-over whenever you groom or pet him and following up with your veterinarian on anything out of the ordinary. Early detection is crucial.

Obesity

One of the most common issues adult dogs face is obesity. Just as with most humans, a dog's metabolism slows with age. Even if your adopted dog is eating the same amount of food and getting the same amount of exercise as he did as a younger pet, he may still be packing some unwanted pounds. If so, your vet may suggest cutting back on his kibble or swapping to a weight-loss formula, as well as increasing his level of exercise.

If your dog is truly obese, you may need to work on the former part of the plan for a while before increasing his activity level. Helping your dog lose the excess weight will be a time-consuming process, but it will be worth your effort. Being overweight increases his risks for a number of diseases, including arthritis and diabetes. By keeping him within an acceptable weight range, you will help him live a longer, more comfortable life.

GERIATRIC CARE

Early preventive care will help ensure that your adopted dog lives a long, enjoyable life, but even the healthiest dogs often face specific challenges as they age. The old claim that one dog year equals seven human years has been refuted many times. Smaller breeds in particular surpass this outdated comparison; some can live well into their teens or even early twenties. As your dog gets older, prevention continues to be his best defense against serious conditions that can interfere with his longevity. Just as with people, healthy pets tend to age more slowly than those that lead unhealthy lifestyles.

If a nutritious diet and exercise are part of your dog's daily life, he will likely act youthful for a long time. Likewise, even a young dog can appear elderly if not kept in proper health. There are no guarantees that disease will not befall a well-cared-for dog, but preventive care will help his chances with whatever might lie ahead.

Older dogs often show signs of their years. The coat of a mature dog may become thinner and drier as he ages, and hair around the face and ears will turn gray. The lenses in the eyes may become cloudy, with a blue-gray appearance. In addition to the aesthetic signs of aging, your dog's hearing will deteriorate as he ages, sometimes resulting in total

If a nutritious diet and exercise are part of your dog's daily life, he will likely act youthful for a long time.

deafness. Heart, liver, and kidney functions tend to become less efficient. The immune system is also less able to fight off bacteria and viruses. Occasionally, incontinence can become an issue. For these reasons, owners of older dogs should increase the frequency of regular veterinary checkups to twice a year. Your vet may also suggest adding blood tests to the routine at this time to monitor various organ functions.

Arthritis

As a dog enters his senior years, he may develop soreness in his joints called arthritis. This will usually be most apparent when your dog moves from lying down to standing or when walking up stairs, but it might also be noticeable during cold, damp weather. Slowing movement is a chronic sign of arthritis, one of the most common afflictions among elderly dogs.

Literally inflammation of a joint, arthritis can strike at any age, particularly after an injury in the areas where scar tissue may be present. Arthritis is more common in overweight dogs, but it can also occur as a result of genetics, targeting an animal's weakest areas. For a small breed like the Boston Terrier, this vulnerable area might be the knees; for a Lab mix it may be his hips.

Many different medications are available to ease the pain of arthritis, but first careful diagnosis is imperative. Once your veterinarian has established that your dog is indeed suffering from arthritis (with the use of X-rays), she may prescribe an anti-inflammatory medication. Certain dietary supplements may also be recommended, particularly glucosamine and chondroitin. Acupuncture also has been found helpful in many cases.

You will be instructed to help your dog lose any excess weight and incorporate a reasonable amount of exercise into his routine. One of the most important steps in managing this chronic condition, lowering your dog's weight also lowers his risk for future injuries that can compound the problems of arthritis.

Patience will also be a large part of helping your senior dog. Once arthritis sets in, it may take him a little longer to get up and move. You mustn't rush an arthritic animal because this can only make further injury more likely. Similarly, you will need to be attentive to your dog's exercise needs while making sure that he doesn't overdo it.

Hypothyroidism

Another condition prevalent among older dogs is an endocrine disorder called hypothyroidism. A dog's thyroid consists of two butterfly-shaped lobes located in the neck. The hormone these lobes secrete is responsible for maintaining the dog's metabolism, the rate at which the body processes its nutrients. In dogs with hypothyroidism, this gland is underactive, consequently slowing the metabolism and making it easier for him to gain weight. Quite often, a dog is predisposed to hypothyroidism. The condition is most common in larger breeds.

If your dog has put on some weight, you must not assume that the thyroid gland is the cause of the problem. If his food intake has not increased along with his weight, however, you may want to look for other symptoms. Has your dog experienced any hair loss or dry skin? Does he always seem to be cold, seeking out warmer places to rest? Does he seem lethargic or depressed? Have ear infections been a problem? These are all signs that the weight gain may be related to a thyroid issue.

If you suspect that your dog is suffering from hypothyroidism, schedule an appointment with his veterinarian. Although the condition is rare in smaller dogs, it can beset any dog. Most dogs will show symptoms between the ages of 4 and 10. Your vet will use a series of tests to diagnose hypothyroidism. Once diagnosed, your dog will need to take a synthetic thyroid hormone to help adjust his metabolism. Periodic blood samples will then need to be drawn to assess the effectiveness of the treatment and make any necessary adjustments.

Treatment is usually extremely successful. Most dogs treated for hypothyroidism return to their normal weight and activity level quickly once treatment is begun. Although regular followup appointments will be necessary to monitor the hormone dosage, your dog should remain symptom-free for the rest of his life and will have the potential to live just as long as a dog without a thyroid problem.

Canine Cognitive Disorder

Similar to human Alzheimer's disease, canine cognitive disorder (CCD), also called cognitive dysfunction syndrome (CDS), can present symptoms much like those of senility. As your dog gets older, it may be more and more difficult to distinguish between CCD and the normal signs of aging. There is one difference between the two, though, that makes differentiation especially important. Unlike senility, CCD is treatable. CCD can also affect a dog of any age, not just an elderly one.

Normal signs of aging may include a gradual loss of mobility, reduced immune system functioning, a slowing metabolism, loss of muscle and bone mass, and reduced functioning of the senses. A dog suffering from CCD will appear less aware of his

Canine Depression

Settling into a new home can take some time, but if your dog doesn't seem to be adjusting after several weeks, you may want to talk to his vet about whether he could be depressed. Although many pet owners think that clinical depression is a condition that strikes only people, pets too can suffer from this debilitating problem. Understandably, losing his home can leave a dog feeling profoundly sad. Also, as with people, dogs can suffer from depression resulting from a chemical imbalance in the brain.

If your dog seems uninterested in daily activities like eating, playing, or going for walks—and these symptoms last for more than a week—he may be depressed. Treatments for canine depression range from behavioral approaches (increased physical activity, socialization, even enrolling your pet in doggy day care) to pharmacological intervention. Prescription antidepressants, as well as natural supplements, are both commonly used to treat canine depression. Once your dog has been diagnosed, your vet can help you create the best treatment plan for him.

surroundings, less capable of learning or adapting, and even unable to remember simple things. Frequently, housetraining is one of the first things forgotten. In addition, CCD affects an animal's behavior and temperament, often straining the relationship between the dog and his family.

Because CCD shares many symptoms with other common canine illnesses, your veterinarian will need to perform several tests—including blood work, urine analysis, X-rays, and a neurological examination—to rule out these other possible causes of the problem. CCD can exist along with other illnesses, making diagnosis especially challenging in these cases. There is currently no cure for CCD, but prescription medications that enhance dopamine levels in the brain can help to minimize symptoms and offer a dog a better quality of life.

Making Your Older Dog Comfortable

Owners can do several things to make their dogs' lives more comfortable as they age. If your adopted dog's eyesight is failing or he tends to stumble frequently, a baby gate will prevent him from falling down the stairs. It can also protect your carpeting if your dog has become incontinent or forgetful of housetraining. If your dog doesn't already have one, an orthopedic bed may be a good idea at this time.

Gray hairs won't bother your dog, but itchy dry skin will. To stimulate the natural oils in his skin, try brushing his coat more frequently. This can also serve as an excellent opportunity to check for fleas and ticks, parasites your older dog will have a harder time fighting. Use care near any of the normal lumps or bumps your dog may have at this stage of life because harsh bristles can hurt.

Welcoming your adopted dog into your home marks the beginning of your new life together. By acting purposefully, you can help make his transition an easier one, but never forget that there are many days still ahead of the two of you. Continued care ensures that these days turn into months and years of good health and happiness.

C h a p t e r

7

TRAINING—
or Retraining—Your Dog

D ogs surrendered to animal shelters and breed rescue groups arrive with a full range of training needs. Many have been housetrained by their previous owners; others have not. Some know a handful of useful obedience commands; many others were never taught how to walk on a leash. Some dogs have been socialized properly; others bark the moment they see people. Your adopted dog may fall on one end of this spectrum or the other, or anywhere in between. As his new owner, you are responsible for picking up where his previous caregivers left off, wherever that may be.

Some owners think of dog training as something they must do for a fixed period of time—that once they have trained their dogs, they will remain trained. The truth is that to be successful, training must be an ongoing task. As owners, we are in fact always training our pets by reinforcing numerous behaviors in one way or another.

Some dogs in need of new homes were surrendered because they didn't make it as show dogs or obedience competitors. These dogs can make wonderful pets, but they may have been treated poorly in the past when they didn't measure up to their previous owners' expectations. This can leave them resistant to the training process; however, a positive approach and patience can make a huge difference.

You owe it to your adopted dog, your family and friends, and the community in which you live to train your new pet. By postponing training until a point at which the task might be more convenient for you, you do your dog and everyone else a great disservice. Waiting to start training until your dog has had a chance to settle in is also a big mistake. While you wait for your schedule to become less busy or for your dog to acclimate to his new home, he will be establishing his own habits.

Just as people continue to learn new things throughout their lives, dogs also keep learning as they get older. No matter what your adopted dog's age or history, he will continue learning all his life whether you train him or not. If you put off training (as your dog's previous owner may have done), your dog will be more likely to learn unpleasant behaviors on his own. By making training a priority from day one of your

For best results, keep training sessions short and end them on a positive note.

new life together, however, you help ensure that what he learns makes him a well-behaved pet.

THE IMPORTANCE OF POSITIVE TRAINING

Positive training is important for any dog, but it is especially crucial for a dog who has suffered the loss of a home and family. Your adopted dog may worry that, like his previous owner, you will abandon him if you are displeased with his behavior. This can make training more difficult for your adoptee, but it makes it even more imperative that training is a rewarding experience. You also can make training less stressful for both of you by setting reasonable goals and avoiding harsh corrections.

Dogs with a history of abuse respond especially badly to punishment, but no dog should ever be punished for any reason. In addition to being cruel, punishment has been repeatedly shown to be an ineffective means of training. Both clinical and anecdotal evidence shows that punishing an animal only teaches him to fear the punisher.

On its most basic level, dog training is about communication. Owners use training as a means of telling their pets what they expect from them. When these instructions are communicated successfully, the dog responds by showing his owner that he understands by complying.

Learning to communicate properly with your adopted dog can keep him safe. You may not be able to teach him that, while chasing butterflies is perfectly harmless, chasing a bumblebee can lead to a trip to the vet's office, but you can tell him to leave a stinging insect alone. You might not be able to make him understand that if he runs into the street, he could be hit by a moving vehicle, but you can tell him to come to you if you accidentally drop his leash while walking him.

For training to be successful, give your dog motivation to listen to you. This is another reason why a positive approach is so important. Positive training means rewarding your dog for what he does right. If he is only showing marginal success toward your goal, reward him for every step he makes in the right direction and continue working with him. This creates a pleasant environment in which your dog is given the tools for continued success.

Motivation and Rewards

Positive training means using rewards, but these can come in a variety of forms. You may choose to use edible rewards when training your dog, a great incentive for most animals. Just be sure they are bite-sized so that they don't distract your dog from the task at hand. Whatever your chosen reward type, never forget to offer heartfelt praise along with it. This, more than anything else, will show your dog that you are pleased. Praise can be the most effective means of getting a dog to repeat a desired behavior.

Training Sessions

Work on one command at a time, and keep your training sessions short—no more than 15 minutes each. At first, just 5 minutes may be plenty. Watch your dog for signs that he's had enough. A wandering attention span is usually a reliable indicator of this. Whenever possible, end on a positive note while your dog still appears interested in the task at hand. Training for short periods of time several times each day is not only less stressful for all involved, but it also typically produces better results than one long training session.

You can train your dog any time of the day, but you may find that he is the most motivated before meals. You can even use

Using Positive Reinforcement

For your pet, positive reinforcement may include food treats, praise, petting, or a favorite toy or game. Food treats work especially well for training. A treat should be enticing and irresistible to your pet. It should be a very small, soft piece of food so that he will immediately gulp it down and look to you for more. If you give him something he has to chew or that breaks into bits and falls on the floor, he'll be looking around on the floor, not at you. Small pieces of soft commercial treats, hot dogs, cheese, or cooked chicken or beef have all proven successful. Experiment a bit to see what works best for your pet. You can carry the treats in a pocket or fanny pack. Each time you use a food reward, you should couple it with a verbal reward (praise). Say something like, "Good dog," in a positive, happy tone of voice.

(Courtesy of the Humane Society of the United States)

All Owners Make Mistakes

Of course, you want to do everything right for your adopted dog, but the reality is that every owner will make at least some mistakes. Whether it's as simple as forgetting to get your dog to his potty spot on time or losing your patience and yelling at him when he chews up the television remote, I promise you are not alone. Admitting our mistakes is important so that we don't repeat them, but dwelling on them won't do us or our dogs any good. When you make a mistake, correct it, and then move on.

your dog's kibble as his edible reward. If dog food doesn't inspire him, try cubed chicken or sliced hot dogs. Just lessen the amount of dog food you give him at meal time to compensate for these goodies.

You will get the best results from training if your dog is calm when you work with him. A calm dog can listen and learn more easily than one who is overly excited or distracted. Training can be a fun and stimulating activity for both people and pets, but if your dog responds to your enthusiasm for the task with frenzied behavior, try to lower your own level of excitement. Use a friendly yet relaxed tone of voice, and try not to move around too much. This will help to create a controlled and productive training atmosphere.

Exercising a dog prior to training is a great way to let him burn off any excess energy. If your dog has a tough time transitioning from playtime to training time, try choosing separate areas for these two different activities. Ending with a second play session—in the designated area, of course—is an ideal way to reward him for his progress.

Once your dog complies with a particular command about 85 percent of the time, continue working on it with him, but begin using the edible reward only intermittently. This part of training, called shaping, ensures that your dog will follow the command whether a food reward is offered or not. As soon as he dependably complies with the task at hand, you can move on to teaching him a new one.

If your mood is poor, postpone training until you can approach the activity with a positive attitude. Dogs are extremely sensitive individuals. They know when their owners are upset, but they can easily misunderstand the reasons. You may have had a bad day at work, but your dog may perceive your annoyance to mean that you are displeased with him. This can send mixed messages in training. Your voice may be telling your dog he did well, but if your heart isn't in it, he will sense this and be less likely to repeat the behavior. For this same reason, if you feel yourself becoming frustrated during a training session, end it as quickly as you can, preferably on a positive note. Return to training once you have had a chance to rest and recharge.

WHEN TO USE A PROFESSIONAL TRAINER

You may wonder if you should go it alone when it comes to training your adopted dog or enlist the help of a professional trainer. The answer depends on two things: your adopted dog's training needs and your level of experience with this kind of training. If he has encountered problems relating to training in the past, seeking the advice of a professional may be smart, even if you have successfully trained your other dogs in the past.

Think of professional training as an investment in your dog's future. Every trainer will have a slightly different approach, so even if you have attended a training class previously, you can still learn something new from a different instructor. If you walk away from a training course with just one new training technique that works well for your adopted dog, you have already received a return on your investment.

For many dog owners, the easiest way to commit to training is by signing up for a class. Even people with hectic schedules can usually fit a weekly class into their routines. They are also more likely to follow through with training both in class and at home if they know they will be attending these regular sessions with others. Training classes also provide a certain amount of camaraderie that many adoptive owners find helpful.

Before signing up for a class, ask how

If your dog has encountered problems relating to training in the past, it may be best to seek the advice of a professional trainer.

Should You Change Your Dog's Name?

Many dog trainers disagree as to whether an adopted dog's name should ever be changed. Perhaps you've always wanted to name a dog Jack, but the gorgeous Golden Retriever you end up finding is already named Buster. Is there any harm in changing it? The answer lies in the details. First, consider your pet's age. If he is still young, he may readily accept a new name. An adult dog, however, may have a harder time accepting this change. Also, consider Buster's history. If he was abused, he may have formed a negative association with his own name. Watch your dog closely when you say his name. Does he lift his ears and wag his tail? If so, he is probably pretty comfortable with his present name. If he ducks his head or tucks his tail between his legs, though, it is likely that his name was used as a punishment in the past. In this situation, renaming him could mark the beginning of his new life with you. If you simply like the name Jack better than Buster, though, it might be best to leave well enough alone. In general, err on the side of caution when it comes to this issue. Unless there is an obvious reason for a change, allow an adopted dog to keep his name. Adopted dogs have already lost so much. If we can let them keep their names, why not?

many dogs will be part of each group. Just like a school for human children, the lower the number of canine students per class the better. This helps ensure that the trainer will have adequate time to answer everyone's questions and offer individual attention when necessary. Also, ask how many family members may attend each class. Involving your entire family in the training process is ideal, but you may have to do so at home if classroom space is limited.

The title "dog trainer" is a bit of a misnomer. Yes, most instructors are skilled dog trainers, but the real purpose of a trainer is to teach the dog owners themselves how to train their pets. In this way, a trainer is really more of a teacher. Never send your dog to a trainer; you should always be an active participant in the training process. A trainer should be friendly and have a good rapport with your dog, but equally important, she must be willing to answer any questions you may have without talking down to you.

Beware of any trainer who promises results in a specific amount of time. Offering a money-back guarantee if you are not satisfied is admirable, but no one can predict how long it will take your adopted dog to learn the commands being taught. It could take six weeks, or it may take six months.

Your veterinarian should be able to suggest a reputable dog trainer in your area. You also can contact the Association of Pet Dog Trainers at (800) PET-DOGS or search their website at www.apdt.com for the name of a trainer near you. Avoid using the phone book or bulletin board advertisements. Dog trainers vary tremendously in both their experience and specialties. They also do not have to be licensed to perform the work they do, so owners must use extreme care in the selection process. If you do select someone without a recommendation, ask for references, and be sure to follow up by checking them.

Look for someone who has worked with dogs similar in size and temperament to your own. If the majority of a trainer's experience has come from working with Chihuahuas and other toy breeds, this may not be the best person for your Old English Sheepdog, and vice versa. Also, if your dog is past the puppy stage, the trainer you choose should have experience working with adult dogs.

While many trainers readily include edible rewards in their protocols, others feel strongly that praise is the only reward a dog needs. Some trainers swear by clicker training, a method that involves reinforcing desired behaviors by making a quick sound with a small, plastic device called a clicker. Whatever approach a trainer utilizes, it should be positive in nature. If a trainer advocates punishment of any kind, take this as a sign that you should continue your search.

SOCIALIZATION

By socializing your dog, you make his life easier. Friendly pets are welcome far more places than shy or belligerent ones. In addition to opening doors for your pet, a social nature helps him feel at ease in virtually any situation. Socializing your adopted dog can be one of the easiest things you can do for him. Simply take him with you to as many places as you can, and introduce him to

Dogs can benefit from socialization at any age.

Communicating With Your Deaf Dog

Training a dog who cannot hear isn't much different than training any other dog. You can even attend conventional training classes with your new hearing-impaired friend along with other owners and their dogs who can hear. One adjustment you will need to make is using hand signals for communicating with your pet. Many owners teach hand signals whether their pets can hear or not. This ensures that a dog will respond even in a noisy setting. Select a unique gesture for each command that you teach your dog. If you have a hard time thinking of an appropriate signal, ask the class instructor for help or buy a book on American Sign Language. Because your dog cannot hear audible praise, remember to use a visual cue for this as well. Clapping your hands can work well. Your facial expressions will also tell your dog when you are pleased, so remember to smile, too!

as many people as possible. If parents ask if their kids can pet your dog, say yes. Just be sure they are old enough to understand that dogs must be treated gently. A bad experience with a poorly behaved child can leave your dog thinking that all kids are mean creatures to be feared.

If you adopt an older dog, or even a younger adult, you may worry that the window of opportunity for socializing him has already closed. While it's true that dogs are the most open to being socialized between the ages of 4 and 12 weeks, adult dogs with sound temperaments can benefit from being exposed to people at any age. You may have to work a little harder at this task than the owner of a puppy, but I assure you this will be time and effort well spent.

If your dog becomes frightened or shy around new people, do not try to soothe or reassure him by petting him or saying things like, "It's all right." Your dog will misinterpret these actions as praise for his reluctant behavior. Instead, continue to expose him to new people, praising him only when he makes a move in the right direction—toward others.

Expose your dog to as many different types of people as possible: men, women, children, elderly people, people of different races, people with disabilities, tall people, short people, men with facial hair, women in hats, people in uniforms, people who wear glasses. The more your dog deals with diversity, the more comfortable he will be when he encounters someone or something new.

Whenever you head out the door with your dog, take along a small bag of treats or pieces of kibble, and ask each of his new acquaintances to offer him one. This will help him form a positive impression of people. But don't limit his exposure to human friends. Let him meet other dogs as well—as long as he has had all his necessary shots and boosters. Always use caution when allowing interactions between your dog and other animals. Ask the owners if their pets are friendly before approaching, and keep a close eye on both animals' reactions as you let them move slowly toward each other while on leashes. If you take your dog to a dog park, do not allow him off his leash—not even for a minute—until you are sure of his temperament in such a setting.

Take your dog with you to the farmer's market, your kids'

baseball games, sidewalk art shows, and other interesting places. If a neighbor invites you to a cookout, ask if you may bring your dog along. If you have friends with dogs, invite them to your own home for canine play dates. Let your dog join you when you have to run errands. Federal law prohibits pets from entering buildings like banks and post offices, but you can always use the outdoor ATM and drop your letters in the outside mailbox so that you have the opportunity to encounter new people along the way. Even if they don't stop to say hello to your dog, just being around them is good for your adopted pet. Never leave your dog unattended in your vehicle, though. Temperatures inside cars, even those with windows left ajar, can skyrocket in just a matter of minutes, which can be deadly for your pet.

While dog-loving strangers may prove to be invaluable in your canine socialization mission, it is important to remember that not everyone likes dogs. Some people, for a variety of reasons, even fear them. If someone prefers not to interact with your dog, don't take it personally. And more importantly, don't push. Instead, respect this person's right to spend dog-free time in public.

A great way to find people and dogs for your new pet to meet is taking him to training classes. Beginner-level classes are

Socialization helps your dog feel at ease in virtually any situation. The more situations you introduce him to, the more comfortable he will be when he encounters someone or something new.

offered in most communities for dogs of all ages. Even if obedience training isn't high on your list of priorities, the social aspects of these lessons alone can make them worthwhile. You may even discover that training is a lot more fun than you imagined.

Like other parts of training, socialization isn't something you should do for a while and then stop. Providing your dog with opportunities to interact with people and fellow pets is something you must continue to do throughout his life if you want him to remain friendly. In addition to being good for your dog's mental health, being social can be fun for both you and your pet.

If your dog shows any signs of aggression—growling at strangers, for instance—socializing him will not be as simple as merely bringing him out to meet the masses. Instead, you must abstain from allowing him around others until you can better assess the situation. In this precarious circumstance, you must consult a professional trainer before moving forward with any type of socialization.

CRATE TRAINING

Crate training is one of the most efficient means of keeping your dog safe when you cannot watch him. By providing him with this simple enclosure, you also offer your dog a quiet place of his own in which to rest, relax, or enjoy a yummy treat. Crates are also extremely useful tools for the housetraining process because dogs have a natural aversion to soiling the area in which they sleep.

With all its advantages, though, the crate is not for every dog. Misuse of the crate can lead a dog to fear being crated or kenneled. Dogs who began their lives in puppy mills and those who were similarly kept in crates for unacceptable amounts of time by neglectful or abusive owners are poor candidates for crate training. For these dogs, the best thing adoptive owners can do is remove the crate from the training equation completely. With the wide variety of safety gates available today, you should be able to create a safe and comfortable space in your home for your dog that will offer him most of the benefits a kennel provides. This is also a great option for owners who simply prefer not to use a crate.

If you do wish to crate-train your adopted dog—and he has no negative history involving a crate or kennel—introduce him to this item the day you bring him home. Ideally, it should be assembled and waiting for him with the door open. Begin by simply allowing your dog to inspect the crate on his own. Place a toy or a few treats inside as enticements, and praise him when he moves across the threshold to get them. Be sure to add more treats for the next time he enters, and continue to praise him each time he does. Whenever you buy your dog a new toy, give it to him in his crate. You may even feed him inside it. This will help him associate the crate with good things.

Once your dog seems comfortable entering his crate, try closing the door for a short period of time. Be sure to give him another treat when you take this next step, both as a diversion from shutting the door and as a reward for tolerating this new phase of his crate training. Only leave the door shut for a minute or two, but be sure not to open it until your dog is sitting quietly. If he fusses or whines, you must wait until he is quiet—even if this is only for a second or two—before touching that handle. This is the point at which some owners encounter

Using a crate is one of the most efficient means of keeping your dog safe when you cannot watch him.

their first experience with resistance from their pets. Be strong. If you give in to fussing, you will teach your dog that this kind of behavior gets him what he wants. You will also make crate training a much more difficult task.

Gradually increase the amount of time you leave the door closed with your dog inside his crate. When he is quiet, you may offer him treats through the door at any time to reinforce this good behavior. Eventually, move out of the room for a short time. This is also a common point for dogs in the throes of crate training to voice their objections. Whenever possible, wait until your dog is quiet before returning to the room and letting him exit the crate. And don't forget to keep the treats coming. Always offer the treats while your dog is still in the crate; you want him to associate the reward with being inside of it and behaving appropriately.

Eventually, you should be able to leave your dog in his crate for longer periods of time while you are in other areas of your home or outside your home. Always remember to give your dog an opportunity to relieve himself before placing him in his crate, and if you've been gone for an hour or more, take him to his potty spot again after letting him back out. Puppies should never be left in their crates for more than an hour or two at a time. Adult dogs should be able to remain crated for four to six hours (or overnight when necessary), but no dog should ever be left in a crate for longer than this. If you work all day, your dog should not be left in his crate for this entire time. If your schedule requires that you be away for the entire day, consider asking a neighbor to stop by or hire a dog walker to give your pet a chance to stretch his legs and eliminate at least once during that long period.

Once your dog has been successfully crate trained, you may then decide to use the crate only intermittently. If he is reliably housetrained and doesn't get into mischief when left alone, there may be no need to crate him whenever you are away or busy. However, use the crate often enough for your dog to remain accustomed to spending time in it—at least a few times a week.

HOUSETRAINING

Housetraining is one of the least pleasant aspects of dog

ownership. I can't think of any pet owner who enjoys cleaning a urine-soaked carpet or accidentally stepping in a pile of dog feces left in the middle of the kitchen floor. Housetraining doesn't, however, have to take long or be as difficult as most people imagine. Even if your adopted dog is beginning this task for the second (or even third or fourth) time,

You can successfully housetrain your dog if you establish a routine and remain consistent.

you can successfully housetrain him if you establish a routine and remain consistent. This is true whether your pet is an older dog or a young puppy.

Never assume that a dog is housetrained, even if the shelter volunteers assure you that he is. The only way to truly know if a dog is housetrained is to live with the animal personally. For this reason, I recommend assuming that any adopted dog is in need of at least some remedial training in this area.

A routine is important, whether your dog is already reliably housetrained or embarking on this journey for the first time. Even a trained animal will have an accident if he is forced to hold his bladder or bowels for too long. It is your dog's job to eliminate in the appropriate place, but it is your responsibility to get him there regularly.

When friends ask me for housetraining advice, the first thing I ask them is this: "How often are you taking your dog to his potty spot?" A young puppy must be taken outside more often than an adult dog, but even adults in the process of housetraining must be taken to their designated bathroom areas religiously every few hours. If you forget to do this, your dog will find another spot out of necessity.

At first, it may seem like housetraining is more about

Track Your Success

Using a chart to help you keep track of your dog's housetraining successes and mishaps can be beneficial. While you certainly shouldn't focus on the accidents, seeing their frequency decrease on paper can be empowering. A chart also can reveal valuable insight—like the times of the day when your dog is most likely to have an accident. Make notes of the times you feed your pet to help remind you when he needs to go to his potty spot. Most dogs need to eliminate about a half hour after eating a meal.

preventing accidents than truly teaching your dog what he needs to do. While this is partly accurate, every time you are able to avoid an accident by getting your dog to his potty spot, you are reinforcing the new habit of eliminating in the proper area. You can't accomplish this important goal without being proactive.

When your dog has an accident—and he will probably have many—you must do three things. First, remove your dog from the area. If your dog has a crate, it will come in mighty handy at this time. If he doesn't, reach for your safety gate, but be sure your dog cannot see you from behind it. If you allow him to witness the cleanup process, you can inadvertently send the message that his role is to make the messes and yours is to clean them up. This too may be partly true, but your dog doesn't have to know this, as it can only make training him more difficult.

Do not reprimand your dog as you remove him from the area of the accident, and never strike him or rub his nose in excrement. Avoid using verbal punishment as well. All that punishment of any kind will accomplish is to confuse your pet, or worse, frighten him. Your dog likely won't understand why you are displeased. If he does link your reaction to what he has just done, he will probably think he is being punished for the actual act of eliminating instead of where he chose to do it. As difficult as it may be, the best thing you can do when your dog has an accident is ignore him completely.

Next, you must thoroughly clean the area where the mishap occurred. Use a rag or paper towel to completely absorb urine before cleaning the area with a pet-safe, scent-eliminating cleanser. Several brands are available at most pet supply stores. If you don't remove every trace of urine, chances for a repeat offense will be higher. Feces too can leave behind an olfactory reminder for your pet, so be sure to clean the area fully even if no stains are left behind once you remove the solid waste.

Finally, when you are done cleaning, take the urine-soaked towel or a small amount of stool to your dog's correct potty spot and leave it right there on the ground. Watch the clock, and as soon as your dog is due to relieve himself again, bring him there. Seeing—and more importantly, smelling—this waste will remind him of why he is there.

Whenever your dog eliminates in the proper spot, praise him

and immediately leave the area. Teaching a dog to eliminate on command will only work when he indeed needs to go, but you can encourage him to do so at these times by teaching him words for urinating and defecating. Whenever your dog begins to urinate, for instance, say, "Go pee." Soon he will associate these words with relieving his bladder. If you merely take him to his potty spot and repeat this phrase over and over in hopes of getting him to go, however, he won't understand what the words mean.

If your dog doesn't eliminate when you take him outside, give him a few minutes and then go back indoors. Watch him closely, and in about 20 minutes, try again. Keep trying until he goes. This can be another grueling part of the housetraining process, especially during cold or rainy weather, but your persistence will pay off eventually. When your dog finally goes, praise him excitedly. You may use edible rewards for reinforcing housetraining success, but the scent of these treats can be distracting for some dogs.

If your dog hasn't eliminated after several trips outside, walking him can help to move his bowels. As your dog walks with you around your neighborhood, he will sniff the grass where other animals have walked recently. In my family, we

Many dogs have pre-elimination habits. Signs that your dog needs to eliminate may include sniffing the ground, circling, or pacing back and forth.

jokingly refer to this as getting e-mail. Your dog will likely relieve his bladder at least once as well as a means of leaving his scent behind for the other animals, which is his reply to their messages.

Although every dog is different, there are certain times when most dogs predictably need to eliminate. These include first thing in the morning, about a half hour after eating, upon waking from a nap, and right before heading to bed at night. While housetraining, it's a good idea to remove your dog's water bowl about one to two hours before bedtime. This can help you avoid overnight accidents, especially if you aren't using a crate. If the weather is extremely warm and your house is not climate-controlled, however, you should leave the water bowl down at all times to prevent dehydration.

Many dogs have pre-elimination habits. Each dog's pre-elimination routine is a little different. Perhaps your dog moves in a circle immediately before going to the bathroom, or maybe he paces back and forth; some do one thing, then another. Many dogs sniff the ground immediately prior to eliminating. If you notice your dog sniffing around indoors, it may be a sign that he needs to go outdoors. Even if you catch your dog in the act of eliminating inside, interrupt him and get him to his potty spot as quickly as possible so that he can finish the task there. By allowing him to finish eliminating inside your home, you reinforce this behavior.

Even if you have a fenced yard, you should bring your dog to his potty spot on a leash while housetraining him, and stay with him until he eliminates. Merely opening the door and telling him to do his business won't work until he learns what this means. Once he is trained, you may let him go outside by himself, but always keep an eye on him so that you're sure he is actually eliminating.

You also can teach your dog to let you know when he needs to visit his potty spot. By hanging a bell or other type of noisemaker by your door, you provide him with a practical way to alert you whenever he needs to go outside. Each time you take your dog out to go to the bathroom, gently lift his paw and tap the bell before heading out the door. If you do this every time you make a potty trip, your dog will see that ringing the bell means he will be let out to relieve himself.

Taking the Right Lead

My dog, Molly, tells me when she has to go outside to relieve herself by coming to me and gently scratching my leg with her paw. When she did this for the first time, I was blown away. I never taught her to do it; she simply developed this habit on her own. Of course, I reinforced the behavior by taking her to her potty spot and showering her with praise when she eliminated. After a while, though, a slight problem developed. Molly would come to me and ask to be taken outside numerous times each day, far more often than she was actually eliminating. It wasn't until she began pulling to leave our backyard that I finally realized what was happening. Molly wasn't just asking to go outside when she needed to empty her bladder or bowels. At least some of these times, she was asking to be taken for a walk.

I was able to differentiate between Molly's two different, albeit related, requests by using a different leash for walks than for taking her to go to her bathroom area. She still uses the same method to get my attention, but when I grab the potty leash, I know in an instant if I have understood her correctly. If she indeed needs to relieve herself, she will sit happily by the door and wait for me to attach this lead. If it's a walk she wants, however, she will have a very different reaction. Everything in her body language will tell me that I'm not on the right track. She will look to other leash and then back at me, sometimes even scratching my leg again.

I now make a point of reaching for a specific leash whenever I head outside with Molly. When I am on a tight schedule and don't have time to take her for a walk before leaving the house, using her potty leash lets her know that she must do her business and then head back inside. When I return from my errands, I will use the leash designated for a stroll around our neighborhood. Using separate leashes for these two different purposes may be helpful for you, too, if your dog has a hard time differentiating between a leisurely walk and a trip outside for elimination. Just remember to always take the right lead.

Training Your Dog to Use a Litterbox

Most dog owners take their dogs outside to do their business, but many owners of smaller dogs prefer to give their pets a place to eliminate indoors. Perhaps you live on the second or third floor of an apartment building, and racing down the stairs to get your dog outside every two hours is more than a little inconvenient. Maybe you work full time and can't make it home midday to walk your dog. Whatever your reason, if you choose indoor training, the process will be very similar to outdoor training with a few obvious differences.

First, you must select the surface on which your dog will be eliminating. Because they are so affordable and convenient, newspapers are a common choice. Paper training has been around for ages, and for good reason: It works. The paper itself is large, absorbent, and relatively easy to remove once soiled. Super-absorbent housetraining pads can also be purchased for this purpose.

Litter boxes, while more common for cats, are growing in popularity among the owners of small dogs. Although they are

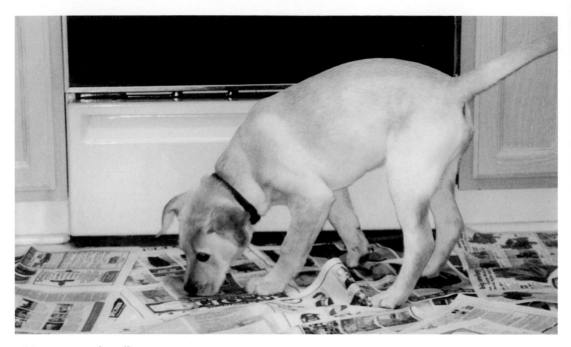

Many owners of smaller dogs prefer to give their pets a place to eliminate indoors. Paper training and using a litter box are common options.

more expensive to set up and maintain than newspapers, they also offer dog owners ease of cleaning and are considered by many to be a more attractive choice. Canine litter boxes, which are larger and deeper than those made for cats, can be found at most pet supply stores. If your local store doesn't carry them, check online.

If you go the litter box route, it is important to know that dog litter and cat litter are not interchangeable. Coarser than the feline variety, dog litter is more absorbent. The biggest problem with using kitty litter for your dog, though, is that many dogs have an inexplicable tendency to eat it, which can be harmful to their health. Neither newspaper nor dog litter really works better than the other in speeding a dog's housetraining success. The medium you choose is really a matter of personal preference.

You will also need to choose a spot in your home for your dog's elimination area. Many people use a corner of the bathroom or kitchen, but really any place without carpeting will suffice. In the beginning stages of housetraining, your dog may not always make it all the way to the litter box, and most floors clean up far more easily than carpeting or rugs.

As you would do if bringing your dog outdoors for

elimination, you should make a point to leave a small amount of urine or stool on the paper or in the litter box initially because this will help remind your dog where he should relieve himself. A dog's sense of smell is so exceptionally sensitive you may find that simply removing the top few layers of newspaper (the ones that become truly saturated) is enough to leave a prompting scent behind. If this doesn't seem to be working, place a saturated sheet just below the new top sheet and toss away the rest.

Dogs being trained for indoor elimination need to be placed on the same schedule as those being taken outside to do their business. The only major difference will be geography. Instead of taking your dog to the backyard, place him on his paper (or in his litter box) whenever he is likeliest to relieve himself, such as after meals, following naps, and the like. When he goes in the proper place, shower him with praise. If he doesn't quite make it to the right spot, remove him from view and discreetly clean up the blunder.

For obvious reasons, a dog trained to eliminate indoors does not need a crate for housetraining purposes (that is, if you want him to be able to relieve himself at will), but there is no rule stating that he can't have one. Your paper-trained dog may actually appreciate the other perks of having a special place of his own. You may also need a crate for traveling with your pet. If your paper-trained pooch does have a crate, just be sure that you occasionally close the door for short periods of time with your pet inside; you want to prevent any negative reaction to doing so when vacation time arrives and shutting the door is necessary.

Changing From Indoor to Outdoor Training—and Vice Versa

In some situations, indoor training is only a temporary decision. For instance, some owners who welcome dogs into their homes in the middle of winter decide to initially paper train their pets and then teach outdoor elimination in the spring. Although this is not an impossible feat, it can be a difficult one. The only thing more difficult, in fact, is training a dog who has previously been trained to eliminate outdoors to relieve himself indoors. Both kinds of transitions are possible, of course, but they will take a great deal of time and effort on the owner's behalf.

If you are trying to teach a previously indoor-trained dog to start eliminating outside, start the same way you would with any other dog, except bring your dog's papers (or litter box) outside with you to the chosen spot. Once he begins to grasp the concept that you are changing the protocol, you can remove these items. However, having them there initially is vital to his understanding of your wishes. Likewise, if you are trying to transition you pet from being an outdoor dog into becoming an indoor dog, bring the papers or litter box outdoors, but in this case you will want to start gradually moving them closer and closer to the door once he begins using them. Your final step in this case is bringing the papers or litter box all the way inside to their permanent location indoors.

BASIC COMMANDS

You may not care if your adopted dog ever wins an obedience title, but teaching him a few basic commands will help ensure his safety and the safety of everyone he encounters. Basic obedience training serves as an effective foundation for all future learning. The most commonly taught obedience commands are *sit*, *down*, *stay*, and *come*. Teaching your dog just one of these commands can take time and a considerable amount of repetition, so be patient and consistent. Like a child, every dog learns at his own pace. Approach each training session with a positive attitude, and don't forget to reward your dog for every step he makes toward these goals.

Basic obedience commands like the sit-stay are the foundation for good manners and all future learning.

Be sure to time your reward properly. If you offer praise or a treat just before your dog complies with a particular command, you will be reinforcing the wrong behavior. Likewise, if you give your dog the reward just afterward, he will associate the treat with whatever he is doing at that moment, instead of with the desired behavior. Also, never use a treat to coax a dog into following your command. A reward should be given only when he is in the process of complying with your instructions.

Many trainers recommend making dogs earn everything they receive as a means of instilling command recall and overall polite behavior. In practical terms, this means making your dog earn treats, toys, even his dinner by performing one or more commands. Before you give your dog his food at mealtime, instruct him to sit. Likewise, command your dog to sit before you open the door whenever heading outdoors. If you have a new toy or treat for your pet, make him to sit, lie down, or stay for a certain period of time before offering it to him.

Watch

Teaching your dog the *watch* command is the most effective means of retaining his attention during all future training. To begin, hold a treat near your face as you say your dog's name. Your dog should respond by looking at you, which is what you want, but wait to reward him until he continues to focus his attention on you a bit longer. Once several seconds have passed, offer him the reward along with copious praise.

Each time you practice the *watch* command with your dog, wait a little longer before rewarding him. If he becomes distracted, put your hand holding the treat behind your back. Seeing the treat disappear may help renew his interest. Once you have recaptured his gaze, you may then dispense the treat after a short wait. Many trainers recommend beginning each training session by practicing this command, which reminds your dog that paying attention truly pays off.

Sit

One of the easiest things to teach any dog is the *sit* command. Many adopted dogs already know how to sit, but if yours does not, this is another great command to start with because sitting is the basis for teaching numerous other commands. Holding a treat in your closed hand, place the hand just above your dog's nose. As your dog moves his nose toward the treat, lift your hand slightly up and over his

head. This will naturally encourage your dog to shift his weight onto his haunches, moving himself into the sitting position. Once your dog sits, say the word *sit* as you open your hand and offer the treat.

Practice this command often and in a variety of places so that your dog becomes accustomed to sitting whenever and wherever you say the word. Be sure to spend at least some time working near the main entrance of your home, though, because this will make it easier to get your dog to comply even with the excitement of a visitor's arrival.

Down

The *down* command follows the *sit* command. It can be especially useful for helping your dog stay out of trouble, particularly when a person or another dog is approaching.

With your dog in the sitting position, hold a treat in front of him, then slowly lower your hand in front of his paws. When your dog lowers his body to get the treat, say the word *down* as you offer both the treat and verbal praise. Once your dog is easily moving into the down position as a response to your moving hand, start issuing the *down* command just before you show your dog the treat, and begin gradually limiting how far you lower or extend your hand. This will help wean your dog from depending on the visual cue.

Stay

The *stay* command is very important for keeping your dog safe. Tell your dog to stay whenever your doorbell rings, for example, to prevent him from running out the door when it opens. The *stay* can also be helpful when entertaining a visitor who is uncomfortable around dogs.

Once your dog can reliably sit when told, you can begin working on the *stay* command. Expect younger dogs or those with short attention spans to remain still for only a second or two at first; this duration will increase over time with work.

After instructing your dog to sit, raise your hand in a stop-sign gesture while saying the word *stay*. Take a step back, and then return to your dog, providing a treat and praise. Make sure your dog does not stand or move as you present the

Adjusting Your Training Approach to Suit Your Dog

Training is definitely not a one-size-fits-all activity. The more you work with your dog, the more you will see how his individual personality (as well as your own) affects your success. Before a particular training technique works for your dog, you may need to tweak it a bit. One of my own dogs seemed to have a hard time learning the *stay* command until my husband began telling her to wait instead. In Molly's case, we think the hard consonant at the end of the latter word resonates with her better than the softer sound of *stay*.

If your adopted dog was abused by a previous trainer, you may want to expand on our strategy. Your dog may have attached a bad connotation to the word *heel*, for example, if his previous owner used it as he yanked on his leash or pushed his back end into the sitting position. In this situation, you may have more success using a different word such as *stop*, for instance. Whatever word you choose, you must use it consistently for your dog to learn what it means.

Sometimes even a well-intended trainer may suggest an approach that just doesn't feel right to you. You might not even know at first what it is about the method that is wrong for your pet. Listen to your instincts at these times, as in so many other areas of pet ownership. Likewise, use what works for you from this book and any other, and forget the rest. By paying attention first and foremost to our dogs' reactions, we learn what does and doesn't work for them. In many ways, they teach us how to train them.

treat because this will reward the wrong behavior. Likewise, don't say the word *stay* unless your dog is indeed sitting still.

When your dog is able to sit for a few seconds, begin gradually increasing both the number of steps you take away from him and the amount of time before offering the reward. Your ultimate goal is for your dog to remain sitting and still for about a minute or longer with you at least 10 feet (3 m) away.

Come

The best way to start teaching your dog the *come* command is by praising him whenever he does it naturally. If you spot your dog in the act of coming your way, say the word *come* in an upbeat tone, followed by excessive praise. It is paramount that you never scold your dog after commanding him to come to you, no matter what he might have done. By following this very important rule, you will help ensure that he will always come to you when called, even when he may be in the midst of a scary situation.

When you are ready to begin working on this command more directly, make sure your dog is on a leash or that you have another individual available to gently lead your dog to you when necessary. Extendable leashes work extremely well for this purpose. Whether you prefer using a leash or a partner, you simply must have a way of getting your dog to follow the command if he doesn't promptly do so on his own.

Heel

Teaching an adopted dog to walk on a leash can take some time, especially if he has never been exposed to this common training tool. For a dog who is afraid of the leash, begin by allowing him to inspect this item on his own for a short time before trying to attach it. Once you hook the leash to your dog's collar, let him walk around wearing it inside your home for a while. Only do this when you can properly supervise your pet, though, so that you can be sure he doesn't choke or strangle himself if the leash becomes caught on anything. Also, be sure to block off any stairways so that he can't trip over the leash and fall down the steps. Some owners attach their dogs' leashes to their own belts, moving through the house with their dogs in tow, so to speak, to help them get used to wearing a leash. This tethering method also can be useful for keeping an eye on your dog during housetraining.

For dogs who pull when walking on a leash, teaching the *heel* command is imperative. The beauty of this command is that, once properly taught, you hardly ever have to say the actual word anymore. What heeling basically means is walking on a leash politely, never pulling, and sitting patiently whenever the person holding the leash stops.

You may be tempted to skip teaching this command, especially if you already use a head harness on your dog. I promise, though, that teaching a dog to heel is not as complicated as it may sound. Head harnesses are extremely effective for preventing dogs from pulling, but only while the dogs are wearing them. When you return to using a conventional leash, your dog almost certainly will resume pulling if you don't teach him the proper way to walk on leash.

To teach the *heel* command, it's best to use a proven training method called "task analysis." By breaking down any multi-part task into smaller, more manageable steps, a dog learns each one separately and can then more easily put them all together toward the final goal. This helps set your dog up for success.

If you don't use a head harness and your dog pulls while

Teaching an adopted dog to walk on a leash can take some time, especially if he has never been exposed to this common training tool.

being walked, simply stand still. Most dogs will turn around to see why their owners have stopped; this also effectively interrupts the pulling. Resume walking, continuing to stop whenever your dog pulls you. If your dog keeps pulling repeatedly, change your direction to show him that it won't get him where he wants to go. Even if you walk your dog on a conventional leash, constant pulling can hurt your dog's throat and also can injure you, so it is extremely important that you correct this problem, even if you have no plans to teach him the full *heel* command.

The next-to-the-last step in teaching your dog to heel is issuing the *sit* command whenever you stop during a walk. Be sure to stop at different points on your route each time. Finally, with your dog's leash in your right hand and a treat in your left, say the word *heel* as soon as your dog sits, and then immediately offer the edible reward along with praise. Timing is crucial for this important last step.

At first, you will need to issue the *sit* command before the *heel* command. After some practice, however, your dog will respond to the word *heel* alone. Eventually, he will freely stop and sit whenever you stop walking. Once your dog has mastered heeling in his own neighborhood, venture out to different places for practice. Teaching your dog to follow commands in unfamiliar environments and amid new distractions is a true training accomplishment.

Drop It / Leave It

The best tool for teaching the *drop it* and *leave it* commands is your dog's favorite toy. He must be wild about the item in order for the training to be most effective. To get started, offer your dog the toy and encourage him to play with it. Once he is immersed in the sound of the squeaker or the taste of mint on his dental chew, pick the item back up as you say the words *drop it*. At first he may not want to relinquish the item. He may even hold onto it a bit tighter when you reach for it, but some gentle coaxing with an edible reward should change his mind. As soon as he drops the toy, offer the treat and praise him for letting go. Practice this exercise over and over until he readily drops the object. Also use other favorite items so that your dog learns that the command applies to any item he may currently possess. I once saved my dog Molly from eating a human multivitamin that I accidentally dropped onto the floor when I issued the *drop it* command. Her immediate response was to pick it up, but she readily let it fall back to the floor when I used this phrase.

Teaching the *leave it* command is very similar to training a dog to drop a particular item. Instead of giving the toy to your dog, however, set it on the floor near him. As soon as he moves toward the item, say the words *leave it* and offer him a treat for his compliance. As with the former command, repeating the exercise will be necessary. This command is useful for keeping your dog from touching anything he shouldn't, such as that runaway vitamin of mine. Unfortunately, I wasn't quick enough to think of using the *leave it* command in that situation, so this is an excellent example of why teaching both commands is a smart move.

Watch Your Words

A command consisting of a single syllable is often easier for a dog to learn than a longer one. Limit each command you use to two syllables at the most for this reason. It is also very important to be consistent with the words you choose for commands. Using two different commands for the same activity will only confuse your pet.

Also, avoid using your dog's name in conjunction with commands. If you say, "Sparky, sit!" your dog may respond but will associate his name with this activity. If so, this could confuse him when you later say, "Sparky, come!" Even more importantly, never use your dog's name with the word *no* or as part of any reprimand because he may form a negative connotation to hearing you say his name, even under more positive circumstances.

CLICKER TRAINING

First used in the 1940s, clicker training is considered by many dog owners to be a more relaxed and fun approach than traditional command-based training. It is based on a proven scientific method of learning called "operant conditioning." By marking a desired behavior the instant it occurs with a two-toned clicking sound from a small plastic device dubbed a clicker, the trainer reinforces the behavior instantaneously with the sound and then rewards it with a treat. As with other styles of positive training, punishment for failure is never used with clicker training.

A command consisting of a single syllable is often easier for a dog to learn than a longer one.

What separates clicker training most from other forms of conditioning-based training is the timing of the click. Rewards, such as edible treats or praise, are offered directly after a desired behavior, whereas the clicking sound must be made during the desired behavior. Although your dog may initially get distracted by the click and discontinue the behavior, the timing of the sound is paramount. The timing of the treat—all-important in reward-based training—is far less important.

One of the biggest advantages to clicker training is that it helps you catch your dog doing the things you want repeated. The theory is that, in time, your dog will begin showing you the desired behaviors on his own, expecting the click. At this time, you should begin offering a cue for your dog to connect with each behavior. When the dog responds to the cue, you can then offer the click followed by a reward, but only if the behavior happens during or after the cue. So, even though this regimen doesn't focus on commands, you will still be able to train your dog to respond to your instructions.

Another important rule of clicker training is only clicking once (pushing in, then releasing) for every time your dog demonstrates a particular behavior. It is fine to click for a behavior that is only a step toward the final goal, though. This is actually the best way to move your dog closer to your objectives. Eventually, as each behavior is mastered, you will discontinue using the clicker for that task, and begin using it for a new one.

Clicker training is not rocket science, but it is a science, so an instructor can be extremely helpful in showing you the best ways to use this effective technique. Although it may seem counterproductive for a large group of people to gather and make clicking noises all at once, classes are offered in many areas for this kind of dog training. A dog's hearing is so much better than our own that dogs are surprisingly capable of discerning their owner's click from any other.

Training a Blind Dog

If you adopt a dog who has lost his sight, I highly recommend these books: *Living With Blind Dogs: A Resource Book and Training Guide for the Owners of Blind and Low-Vision Dogs* and *New Skills for Blind Dogs*, both by Caroline Levin.

CANINE BODY LANGUAGE

While people rely primarily on words to express their feelings, dogs use body language as their prime means of conveying their moods and emotions to their owners and to each other. Sometimes vocalizations will accompany these gestures, but usually sounds aren't even necessary for accurate interpretation. Many common canine postures exist, each with its own specialized meaning. Paying attention to these gestures can help owners in a number of ways.

If your dog is feeling bored, this may be a practical time to hold a training session. If he is feeling playful, it could be an ideal time to grab his ball instead of his training treats. If he shows signs of feeling angry or agitated, it may not be the best time for socialization. By watching your dog carefully for clues to how he is feeling, nearly any activity can be made easier.

Perhaps the most important thing to remember about canine body language, however, is that the meanings are not always universal. The implication of a particular gesture can vary somewhat from dog to dog. As you get to know your adopted dog, you will become more fluent in his individual body language.

Dogs use body language as their prime means of conveying their moods and emotions to their owners and to each other. This "bow" is an invitaion to play.

Elbows Lowered With Bottom in the Air

Often referred to as the play bow, this most adorable canine stance (which usually includes tail wagging and a good-natured bark) is an invitation for play. Your dog may use this gesture with his human family members or other animals within the home.

Exposed Belly

To show his submissive position, a dog may lie on his back and raise one leg when a more dominant member of the pack arrives. With his ears back and belly exposed, this dog is telling you he is not a threat.

Sleeping on His Back

While your dog's exposed belly indicates submission when he is awake, a dog lying this way before going to sleep is essentially telling you he doesn't have a care in the world. Because lying on his back this way leaves him extremely vulnerable, only a dog who feels completely secure will sleep in this position.

Ears Forward or Back, Tail Straight Up, Teeth Exposed

With or without the teeth exposed, this is an aggressive posture. It also may or may not be accompanied by growling, loud barking, or even snapping. An angry dog will usually hold eye contact challengingly.

Ears Down, Tail Hanging Limp

A dog lying in this position is bored. Perhaps it's time to break out the squeaky toys.

Cowering or Hiding Behind Furniture

If your dog is frightened, he may hide behind or beneath a chair or other piece of furniture. This springs from your dog's natural instinct to seek the safety of his den when danger is present.

When training is done with love and patience, most dogs can learn everything they need to know.

Pay Attention to Your Own Body Language, Too

Whenever you work on training your adopted dog, be aware of what you do with your hands. Dogs pay attention not only to their owners' words but also to their body language. For this reason, it is especially important that you use the same gestures whenever working on a specific command with your pet. If you raise your hand showing your dog your palm whenever you instruct him to stay, for example, you mustn't do this when you issue any other command. If you get your signals crossed, it could interfere with your dog's training success.

TRICKS

In addition to these more practical commands, you can also teach your dog fun tricks such as rolling over, shaking paws, or standing on his hind legs. You can even make up your own tricks. I once knew a dog who answered her owner's telephone on command. When I was a child, I taught my Miniature Poodle to close doors. Teaching tricks can help make training fun and interesting for both you and your pet. And if training time is fun, you will both be more likely to start each session with a positive attitude toward whatever training agenda you have planned.

Because there are so many different aspects to training, it can seem like the hardest part of adopting a dog. Indeed, training is usually the most time-consuming and challenging of all the tasks adoptive owners must assume. That's the bad news. The good news is that as long as you remain consistent, you are free to work at your dog's—and your own—pace. When training is done with love and patience, most dogs can learn everything they need to know.

DEALING
With Problem Behaviors

One of the most intimidating parts of dog adoption is the prospect of dealing with any unpleasant behaviors that your adopted dog has developed before coming home with you. Even dogs with the best temperaments may have a nasty habit of chewing inappropriate items or howling when left alone. Many undesirable behaviors arise largely out of boredom, so providing your dog with plenty of attention and toys is a great way to begin nipping any problem behavior in the bud. Sometimes, though, a problem is more deeply ingrained or serious. In these cases, seeking the help of a professional trainer may be necessary.

EXCESSIVE BARKING OR HOWLING

The best method for reducing excessive barking is good old-fashioned distraction. Music can serve as a wonderful buffer if noises tend to prompt your adopted dog's barking. Placing your dog's crate away from outside walls or windows where people and other sounds can be heard easily can help as well. Socializing your dog may help if he barks mostly when you entertain visitors within your home. In this case, providing him with a special treat that he receives only when visitors are present may be effective.

Many dogs are very good at alerting their owners to the presence of strangers, so this may be the key factor in your dog's barking problem. I am convinced that my two Cocker Spaniels think they own the sidewalk in front of our home. You will not be able to completely stop your dog from barking when he hears a suspicious noise, and you may actually want him to serve in a watchdog role. This doesn't mean that you want prolonged barking, though. To reinforce appropriate behavior in this case, teach your dog the *enough* command.

To teach the *enough* command, you must first teach the *speak* command. You can do this by issuing the command as you knock on any hard surface, hopefully encouraging your dog to bark in response to the noise. Once your dog learns to speak upon command, begin implementing the word *enough* as soon as a break occurs in the barking, rewarding him immediately for stopping. The timing of the command is crucial because you want to issue the command as soon as your dog stops barking;

Undesirable behaviors often arise out of boredom. Providing your dog with plenty of attention and toys is a great way to prevent most common problems.

otherwise, you will end up rewarding the wrong behavior. Whenever your dog informs you of an approaching visitor or other noise, praise him for bringing the sound to your attention. Once you acknowledge the situation, say *enough*. As soon as your dog stops barking, offer a reward. This will ultimately teach him that bringing a noise to your attention is acceptable, but continued barking is not.

Never yell at your dog when he barks. In addition to scaring him, all you will do by raising your voice is confuse him. To dogs, yelling sounds like more barking. If you yell, your dog will think you are joining him in this vocal activity instead of understanding that you want him to stop.

If your dog barks when no one is at home with him, the problem probably stems from loneliness. In the wild, dogs vocalize as a way of bringing the pack together. Domestic dogs also use this technique to reach out to their human family members. One way to keep your dog from feeling lonesome is by taking him with you when you go to places where dogs are welcome. Of course, there will be times when your dog cannot accompany you, but being able to go along as often as possible can ease your dog's feelings of loneliness when he must remain at home.

To make the time your dog spends home alone more enjoyable, invest in some fun toys and yummy treats that he only gets when you are out. These can serve as practical distractions and can also help him form a more positive emotional response to being home without company. Some owners find that leaving a radio or television playing helps to ease boredom, another common factor for dogs who bark excessively when left by themselves. Providing your dog with a canine companion also may alleviate both loneliness and boredom when you must be away from your pet, but this is a big step. Every adopted dog should be wanted in his own right, not merely as a playmate for your first pet.

CHEWING

Inappropriate chewing can be caused by many possible reasons. Teething, anxiety, boredom, and lack of exercise are all potential causes. To avert your dog from using your personal property as chew toys, provide him with a variety of acceptable items for chewing. A dog will be much less likely to chew your things if he has plenty of his own. Toys that present the opportunity for stimulation, such as balls that release treats upon manipulation, can also be helpful in distracting your dog from feasting on your belongings.

Teach your dog a command such as *drop it* or *leave it* for those times when you catch him chewing anything unacceptable.

Attention-Seeking Behaviors

Without realizing it, we often pay more attention to our dogs when they're misbehaving. Dogs who don't receive a lot of attention and reinforcement for appropriate behavior may engage in destructive behavior when their owners are present as a way to attract attention—even if the attention is negative, such as a verbal scolding.

Try these solutions instead:

- Make sure your dog gets a lot of positive attention every day—playtime, walks, grooming, or just petting.

- Ignore bad behavior as much as possible and reward good behavior. Remember to reward your dog with praise and petting when he's playing quietly with appropriate toys.

- Make your dog's favorite off-limits chew objects unattractive or unavailable to him. Use aversive products (such as bitter sprays) on objects that cannot be put away.

- Teach your dog the *drop it* command so that when he does pick up an off-limits object, you can use the command and praise him for complying. The best way to teach *drop it* is to practice exchanging a toy in his possession for a tidbit of food.

- Practice the concept of "nothing in life is free" with your dog. Make your dog earn absolutely everything you give him. Instruct him to sit before giving him his food bowl or opening the door to go for his walk. This gets your dog in the habit of complying with your commands and is a good way to make sure that he gets lots of positive attention for doing the right things. By being recognized for appropriate behavior, he won't have to resort to misbehaving just to get your attention.

(Courtesy of the Humane Society of the United States)

Avoid the temptation to give him an item he has already damaged. Although you may have no further use for it, allowing your dog to keep it will only further confuse him as to what is and isn't fair game. For this reason, also avoid giving your dog old shoes or clothing as toys. When he begins chewing an improper item, remove it from his possession and offer one of his own chew toys as a replacement. Praise your dog when he accepts the substitute.

DIGGING

Digging is another very natural canine behavior, but if your dog is making a compost pile out of your vegetable garden, his digging has become a problem. Redirection is usually the best way to prevent digging. If your dog spends regular time alone in your backyard, provide him with plenty of toys to keep him busy. Even the most ardent diggers would rather play a game of ball with their owners than dig, but playtime doesn't always have to be a joint activity. Tasty bones and balls that dispense treats when rolled the right way can serve as excellent distractions for a dog who tends to dig when he is bored.

Rising temperatures can also prompt digging. Some dogs dig to create a cool rest spot on a hot day. If this is the driving force behind your adopted dog's digging, try keeping him out of the hot sun, and always provide him with plenty of fresh drinking water.

If your catch your dog in the act of digging, redirect him to another spot. Offering him a toy can help him from returning to the scene of the crime. Praise him for his compliance. If he continues to dig, either in the original spot or elsewhere, again move him to a different area and encourage him to participate in a different activity. If he still continues, you have two choices: Bring him indoors, or decide to designate a small section of your yard as a dog-friendly digging zone.

Allowing your dog to dig in a small area of his own is often the most efficient way of solving this problem. True, your dog will still be digging, but by limiting him to this area, you could be saving your garden or lawn. If your dog tries moving beyond this spot, simply redirect him back to his area, praising him for digging only there.

If providing your dog with a place of his own in which to dig isn't an option, you may have to refrain from allowing your dog to spend time in your yard. Most importantly, never leave your dog unattended, even with a secure fence in place. An experienced digger will often have no trouble getting out of the yard by digging a tunnel underneath it.

JUMPING UP

If your dog jumps up on people when he gets excited, you must address the problem swiftly. Of course, not everyone minds being jumped on by a dog, but young children and elderly adults can be hurt easily by a large dog with even the best of intentions. Also, some of your guests *will* mind being jumped on by a dog. For these reasons, it is best to correct the behavior before it poses a problem.

When most dogs jump on people, they are seeking attention. Therefore, one of the best strategies for correcting the problem is withholding attention whenever your pet jumps on you. As soon as your dog jumps up, interrupt him by issuing the *sit*

The Dog Rolled in What?!

Upon returning from a walk with my dog Molly recently, I stopped to chat with one of my neighbors. As I held Molly's leash, I commented on the high volume of seeds that had littered my driveway from a nearby maple tree. When I was a child, my friends and I used to call them helicopters because of the way they twirled through the air as they fell. They seemed less charming to me as an adult. I was not as displeased with the abundance of seeds, though, as I was with what Molly did next. When I looked down, my pretty, long-haired dog, who loves nothing more than having a bath, was rolling in a big pile of the brown helicopters, mixed with a plentiful amount of dirt and other debris from the ground. "Molly, what are you doing?" I asked as I reached down to brush her off, but it made no difference. She continued to roll and roll until I told her it was time to go inside. My neighbor, who knows Molly quite well, thought the whole thing was extremely amusing.

After brushing her off once again before heading indoors, I reminded myself that the situation could have been worse. Many dogs enjoy rolling in much more repulsive substances than tree seeds and dirt. Some will roll in mud, animal carcasses, and even excrement. The reason for this seemingly odd behavior is actually pretty simple. In the wild, wolves and dogs cover themselves in smells like these to mask their own natural scents. This makes it easier for them to approach their prey and also protects them from being identified by predators. Many domesticated dogs have retained this age-old instinctive habit.

Fortunately, Molly hasn't rolled in the dirt since this first (and hopefully last) incident. If your dog does roll in grubby substances regularly, however, the solution to the problem may surprise you. Before heading outdoors with your dog, rub him down with a cloth carrying his own scent. This easy preventive measure helps give a dog confidence about his body scent and lessens his desire to cover it up with other, less pleasant odors. Because many dogs will roll in grass or soil directly following a bath, remember to rub your dog down following bathing as well.

Because most dogs are seeking attention when they jump up on people, one of the best strategies for correcting the problem is to withhold attention whenever your pet jumps on you.

command. When he complies, you may then show your dog some attention once again, but try to limit your animation because your goal is to discourage him from jumping up again.

You can practice reinforcing this by asking a friend to help you. For the best results, select someone whom your dog especially likes. When your friend arrives, instruct him or her to issue the *sit* command the moment your dog jumps up. Repeat this exercise several times during your friend's visit. If your dog has a hard time reeling himself into the sitting position, you may issue the *down* command to help him control himself.

Ask your friends never to tolerate your dog's jumping. People who love animals may often say, "That's okay," and continue greeting your dog whether he's on the floor or in their faces. Explain to them that jumping is a problem for you and that you would really appreciate their help in solving it. When you further explain that favorite friends are the best people who can help, most will oblige and be more than willing to issue a firm *sit* and offer the heartfelt praise that should always follow.

HOUSETRAINING REGRESSION

Occasionally, a previous owner will exaggerate about how well housetrained a dog is when surrendering him. If this is the case, remedial training should solve the problem. Sometimes, however, a dog who has indeed already mastered the housetraining process begins having accidents again. If your dog suddenly begins urinating or defecating in inappropriate areas, make an appointment with your dog's veterinarian to rule out a medical cause, such as a kidney problem or diabetes, because incontinence can be a warning sign of either condition. It is crucial that you make sure the problem is not physical before you decide how to approach the issue behaviorally.

If your dog seems to be fighting a case of diarrhea, the cause is likely something he ate. Dogs are extremely sensitive to even small changes in their diet. Eating something they shouldn't—such as something from the garbage can—can easily make them sick, but so can changing too quickly from one type of kibble to another. Sometimes diarrhea can cause a temporary loss of bowel control. If your dog experiences this problem, refrain from scolding him. Remedial housetraining isn't necessary in this situation either; your dog simply could not make it to the appropriate elimination spot in time. I have found that mixing a little canned pumpkin (plain, no sugar added) into a dog's dry food works wonderfully for relieving diarrhea. Ironically enough, this tip often works for curing constipation as well. After a bout with diarrhea, make sure your dog is getting a sufficient amount of water to prevent dehydration. If the incident is an isolated one, there is no need for alarm, but an ongoing problem indicates a need for veterinary evaluation.

If you notice the presence of blood in your dog's stool, try not to be alarmed. Although this is frequently a sign of serious illness in human beings, it is surprisingly common among dogs and rarely a sign of a terminal condition. It does, however, indicate that a medical issue is present, so do schedule an appointment with the vet. Your dog may be suffering from an infection or a parasite of some kind, or a more chronic condition such as colitis. If your dog has consumed an item with a sharp edge (such as a piece of a bone), there is also a chance that this foreign object has scraped the inside of your dog's large intestine.

It is also necessary to seek veterinary attention if you see signs of blood in your dog's urine. This can be a symptom of a minor urinary tract infection (UTI) or of a major illness such as bladder cancer. Blood in urine will not necessarily appear dark red; there may be only a slight red or pink tinge. If your dog eliminates outdoors, you might not even notice its presence, so an accident inside may actually be a blessing if it calls

If your housetrained dog suddenly begins urinating or defecating in inappropriate areas, it may be because he has a medical problem.

your attention to this issue.

Inspect your dog's urine and feces regularly to stay abreast of any problems before they develop into more serious issues. Contact your vet if your dog has passed bloody stools, dark, tarry-looking stools, or stools containing visible worms or other parasites. You will likely be asked to bring a sample. I try to always bring along a stool sample whenever my dogs visit the vet just as a safety precaution because certain parasites cannot be seen without the aid of a microscope.

Though a bit trickier to collect, a urine sample will be necessary if your dog is passing blood or demonstrating an inability to hold his bladder. Because a free-catch sample is required, you will need to place a clean container (a washed baby food jar works well) under your dog as soon as he begins urinating. If your dog is suffering from a UTI, the collection process will be a bit easier if only because another symptom of this problem is frequent urination, often accompanied by great urgency.

Once a health issue can be ruled out, it may then be time to consider the possibility that your dog's housetraining regression is behavioral in nature. You mustn't, however, confuse submissive urination or excitable wetting with intentional urination. Many dogs tend to leak a bit of urine when excited or when in the presence of a person they consider to be a superior "dog." Both these problems can usually be managed by making a few small changes in your household routine, such as postponing the greeting process after returning home until your dog has had a chance to calm down and relieve himself in the appropriate spot.

Marking is an entirely different issue. Dogs will spray urine in very specific areas with the intention of identifying (or marking) these spots to show ownership. Although more common in male dogs, females are also known to do this. Thoroughly cleaning any areas that have been "claimed" will help prevent further incidents. If the behavior persists, obedience training is often recommended because it will help your dog to better understand his position in your household.

COPROPHAGIA

To the dismay of many adopted owners, some dogs develop a habit of eating their own stool. Many owners, particularly those with weak stomachs, find this to be the very worst of all problem behaviors. Rest assured that if you are facing this problem, there are things you can do to stop it. First, however, you must understand why your dog is doing it.

As unimaginable as it may seem, coprophagy (the technical term for the act of eating feces) is a very common and even somewhat natural behavior among dogs. When a female dog gives birth to a litter of puppies, part of her job is keeping each pup clean. By eating their waste, the dam effectively keeps her den (or whelping box) free of fecal matter and parasites. This instinct is deeply ingrained. Wild dogs also eat the feces of their young as a means of ridding the den of odor to keep predators away.

Domesticated puppies may learn to eat feces watching their mothers do it and continue the behavior into their first year of life. Most dogs outgrow coprophagy on their own, but some don't. Adult dogs who have never eaten feces are unlikely to start unless they see another dog doing it. So, your adopted dog could have picked up the behavior in the shelter environment. Dogs learn many things, both good and bad, from watching each other.

The first thing to consider is whether your dog is getting enough to eat. Well-fed dogs are less likely to eat feces. It is not just the amount of food you must consider, though. Make sure your dog is on the right type of food for him. If he is extremely active, for instance, he may need a high-energy formula dog food. Also, boredom can contribute to a dog's tendency toward stool eating. Provide your dog with tasty chew

Bottom Dragging

If your adopted dog drags his bottom on your floors or carpets, schedule an appointment with his veterinarian. This unpleasant behavior is often a sign of one of two problems. Your dog might be reacting to itching caused by an internal parasite such as worms. You probably won't see any worms in his stool, but they may be present nonetheless. The only way to rule out this problem is by bringing a stool sample to your vet. The more likely situation, however, is impacted anal glands. Dogs, both males and females, have glands (or sacs) on both sides of their anal openings. Usually, these sacs empty themselves every time your dog defecates, but they can fill with fluid if not regularly emptied either naturally or by a veterinarian or other caregiver. Impacted anal glands can be very uncomfortable.

Ask your veterinarian to empty your dog's anal sacs whenever he is seen. Although it can be a rather unpleasant job due to odor, some groomers also provide this service. If not emptied, impacted anal glands can become infected and even rupture.

Occasionally, a dog without worms or impacted glands will drag his bottom. Some dogs do this shortly after moving their bowels. Giving your dog a few minutes before bringing him inside from a potty trip can encourage him to use the grass instead of your carpet for this post-elimination habit.

toys to keep him busy whenever he is alone, including when he is crated, because many dogs possess a strong desire to keep their rest areas clean.

You can prevent coprophagy by removing the temptation—literally. Keep your dog's potty spot pristinely clean. As soon as he eliminates, remove any solid waste from the area immediately. Not only does this keep your dog from eating stool, but it also reduces the amount of bacteria in this spot that your dog visits so often.

If the problem continues despite your best efforts, talk to your veterinarian. Many vets suggest adding fiber to the dog's diet. Fiber changes the consistency of the stool, which often makes the fecal matter less appealing. Digestive enzymes may be added to your pet's food as well to spoil the smell and taste of the stool for your dog. A popular home remedy to combat stool eating is sprinkling meat tenderizer on the food, which acts as a similar deterrent. Although this may work, I advise against it because most tenderizing spice mixes are extremely high in sodium. A better option is to give your dog acidophilus, a probiotic that helps maintain intestinal balance. Consult your vet for the right dosage based on your dog's weight.

BEGGING

Like so many problem behaviors, it is much easier to prevent begging at the table than it is to correct it, but there is still hope if your adopted dog has picked up this unpleasant habit. You may not think of table manners as something you need to teach your dog, but if you plan to dine with him in the room, you must help him behave properly. The primary reason most dogs misbehave when their owners are eating is that these owners frequently give in to their dog's begging. The worst thing you can do if your dog fusses while you eat is share your food with him. By doing so, you are actually teaching your dog to beg—and quite effectively I might add. Once learned, this can be one of the hardest canine habits to break. The key is to break your own habit of giving in to your pet's demands.

To discourage your dog from begging, it is a smart idea to feed your dog his dinner at the same time the rest of your family eats. If you must feed your dog before you eat, consider giving him a tasty chew toy to help keep him occupied while you enjoy your meal. Do not give him table scraps, though, even if he never begs for them because this will surely teach him to beg in the future.

Just because you shouldn't feed your dog from the table doesn't mean that you should never share food with him. On the contrary, allowing him a reasonable portion of a healthy meal—and even serving him his meal alongside the rest of your family—can be an excellent way to show your dog how much you love him. My own dogs would be heartbroken if I were ever to cook corn-on-the-cob without including an extra ear for them. Watching the two of them standing side by side, munching the kernels from the cob as my husband rolls it back and forth for them, is one of my favorite parts of summer, when this vegetable is in season here in New England. The problem arises when a dog begs for food he is not offered. Your dog may do this by vocalizing in a high-pitched whine, using his paws to "remind" you of his presence, or simply sitting and staring you in the face while you eat. While the last behavior (staring) may not bother you as much as the first two, they are all begging behaviors and should never be tolerated.

If your dog begs in any way while you are eating, promptly remove him from the dining area. Even if the bad behavior occurs near the end of your meal, try to give your pet a chance to rejoin you before you have finished eating. His actions at this point will be a good indication of whether or not he learned anything from being remanded to his crate or the other room. If you are consistent in this approach, he will eventually link the begging with his removal.

When sharing food, preparing your dog's portion at the kitchen counter (instead of placing it in his dish from your plate at the table) will help him understand that his food is his and your food is yours. Also, be sure not to share any more food with your dog after he starts begging. Whether the food comes from your plate or the counter, it is imperative that you never reward this behavior.

GETTING INTO THE TRASH

If your adopted dog has a penchant for trash picking, the solution is as simple as taking out the garbage. Avoid putting tempting items in trash containers within your home. Always use the garbage disposal for discarded food, and keep your wastebasket lids closed at all times. If your dog is particularly persistent in his dumpster diving, keep trash containers in closets or cupboards to limit his access.

Scavenging is a natural canine behavior, but some of the items your pet seeks out may surprise you. My own dog, Damon, has never once gotten into my kitchen trash can, but he will inevitably tear a tissue to shreds if he sees even a corner of it protruding from the bathroom wastebasket. For this reason, I have to be especially diligent about emptying my own trash containers, and I never put anything in them that could hurt my pets. Expired medications, for instance, might not be what Damon is looking for, but he could be seriously harmed if he ever consumed any of them before tearing up those tissues.

AGGRESSION

Canine aggression must never be tolerated. Although many factors can contribute to a dog's tendency to bite, none is an acceptable excuse. If only one situation exists for which obedience training is necessary, this is it. Teaching your dog that you are his leader is the most important step in correcting aggressive behavior. If your dog is biting, it may also be wise to consider possible contributing factors such as where your dog sleeps, when he is fed, and what

games you play with him because these things may be affecting your dog's perception of his place in the family.

Playing tug of war games can intensify an aggression problem in an already hostile animal.

If your dog has assumed the alpha role in your household and uses aggressive behavior toward family members as a means of retaining this position, this is a true emergency.

Consult your veterinarian, a canine obedience instructor or dog trainer, or an animal behaviorist immediately for advice on how to solve this very serious problem. Whether your dog weighs more than you do or just a few pounds, he could hurt someone. And in the unfortunate event that he does, you could be faced with a lawsuit or worse—the unimaginable possibility of being legally forced to euthanize him.

If your dog is displaying signs of aggression, a dog park or a day care is not the answer. Only dogs with reliable dispositions should be taken to dog parks. Likewise, day care providers will gladly accept dogs with good temperaments in an effort to curb such behavioral issues as chewing or barking, but they must draw the line at aggression because it puts their other canine clients and staff members at risk. In this case, you should seek the advice of a professional trainer or an animal behavior specialist, but talk to your veterinarian first.

Aggression should always be treated as a serious matter. Even if your dog is only acting aggressively with a certain person or over a particular item, such as his food or a favorite toy, intervention is an absolute necessity. Until you have created a plan for dealing with the problem and you are seeing consistently positive results, do not allow your dog near other people.

Even if your dog displays no signs of aggression whatsoever, never allow him to place his teeth on your skin for any reason. Teething puppies get great satisfaction from chewing on virtually anything they can wrap their tiny chompers around, but even this seemingly innocent gnawing can set a dangerous precedent. Teach your dog that touching others with his teeth is not allowed. If you have children, make sure they too know that biting of any kind is against the rules.

If your dog acts aggressively over his food, begin hand-feeding him immediately. The old saying that a dog won't bite the hand that feeds him can be mighty accurate in a very literal sense. Offer your dog his kibble one piece at a time, and stop immediately if he growls or if he takes the food from you too forcefully. If he hasn't eaten enough, you may begin hand-feeding again after a short break. Your dog will soon learn that acting aggressively means waiting for his dinner.

Never reward your dog for acting aggressively. Playing tug of war games can intensify an aggression problem in an already hostile animal. Allowing your dog to sleep on your bed with you, particularly at the head by your pillows, is also a bad idea if he has shown any aggressive tendencies. If allowed, sleeping on the bed should be a privilege that your dog earns with good behavior.

COMPOUND PROBLEMS

Sometimes an adopted dog displays two or more problem behaviors simultaneously. For instance, your new pet may be barking excessively, chewing inappropriate items, and getting into your trash. If this scenario sounds familiar, ask yourself when these misbehaviors are occurring. If your dog acts out most often when you are not home, he may be trying to tell you that he is bored or lonely. Although the problems may seem numerous, a common solution may be the answer, such as keeping a wide variety of toys on hand. Sometimes multiple problems require individual solutions; in these cases, the advice of a professional may be necessary.

FEAR-BASED PROBLEM BEHAVIORS

Fear-based problems require special approaches. Dogs can be frightened or phobic of people, places, noises, and certain objects. Your dog needn't have had a traumatic experience with something to become frightened of it. Some dogs are just more prone to fearful behavior than others. Although fearful behaviors aren't inherited, a dog's genetic makeup can result in a tendency toward these responses. Fearful behaviors require counter conditioning and desensitization programs, which expose your dog to more tolerable versions of whatever he is afraid of and work to gradually eliminate the stress associated with it.

Fear of Loud Noises

Any dog can suffer from a fear of loud noises, but this problem is particularly common among previously abused pets. If a past owner fired guns or set off firecrackers too close to your dog, or even chased him with a vacuum cleaner or hair dryer, this could have triggered your pet's fear. Even yelling could be at the root of the problem. No matter what type of sound led to the problem, once an animal develops this fear (sometimes called sound shyness), any loud sound can scare him. Your adopted dog may be fearful of the sound your garbage can makes when you roll it down your driveway to the curb, or he may run and hide whenever he hears a motorcycle drive past your home. He may even be frightened by certain sounds from your kids' toys. Many dogs with this problem may become extremely frightened during thunderstorms.

If your dog has a fear of loud noises, one of the best things you can do for him is to keep him away from them whenever possible. For example, crate your dog in another room or have a family member take him for a walk when you vacuum. Close the bathroom door when you dry your hair, and make sure your dog is indoors whenever you take the trash out. Refrain from taking your dog to events where there will be fireworks or loud music playing. Cheering crowds also can sometimes pose a problem for sound-shy pets.

Because you can't control the weather, your dog will need to endure the occasional thunderstorm. You can help

Everyday Fears Versus Phobic Fears

It is very important to know the difference between a mild fear and a more serious, phobic situation. Some fears can be dissolved through repeated exposure and positive reinforcement. Others, however, can cause your dog great mental and emotional distress if you force him to confront them.

If your adopted dog is afraid of people wearing hats, you can probably help him through this minor apprehension. Whenever you venture into public with your pet, bring a container of tasty treats with you and ask anyone you see wearing a hat to offer him one. It shouldn't take long for your dog to willingly approach anyone wearing a hat; he might even start seeking them out!

If your dog acts fearful when in the presence of bigger dogs, don't indulge his trepidation by coddling him or avoiding these other dogs when you see them at the park. Instead, expose him to as many friendly, generously proportioned pooches as you can—just one or two at a time, of course. Again, offer him treats while around these other dogs so that he can attach a positive connotation to being in their presence. He may still act submissively when around these larger animals, lying down and exposing his belly, for example. This is fine, but he doesn't need to fear them.

If, on the other hand, your dog's fear is more deeply ingrained, it may be better to avoid the trigger whenever possible. Dogs who fear loud noises, for instance, do not need to be exposed to overwhelming sounds like gunfire or lawnmowers. If your dog is sound-shy, don't take him hunting with you—no matter what his breed. If your neighbor is mowing his lawn, postpone your dog's outdoor playtime until the lawnmower has been put away. Forcing phobic dogs to face their fears will only exacerbate the problem.

A good way to tell the difference between an everyday fear versus a phobic fear is by first considering how intensely your dog reacts to the situation and then how easily the trigger can be avoided. If your dog fears something that he must be exposed to from time to time—riding in a vehicle, for example—you should try to help him overcome his qualms by taking him with you as often as you can, ideally to fun places he will want to visit again and again. Even healthy pets need to see their vets at least once a year, but if your dog is sick or injured, you will need to transport him to the hospital as quickly as possible. A fear of riding in an automobile will only make your ailing pet more nervous in this situation. If your dog has developed a deep-seated fear of something that you cannot avoid, consult an animal behaviorist for advice on solving the problem.

him through stressful weather-related events by never taking him outdoors when you hear thunder and bringing him indoors immediately if you are out for a walk and the sky starts rumbling. Once inside, close your window shades and try to muffle the sound by switching on a radio or taking your dog to a quieter area of your home, such as a family room in the basement. If you use a crate, this may be an excellent time to place your dog inside his kennel with a tasty treat for distraction because it often serves as a comforting environment to frightened animals. As tempted as you may be to console your dog during a storm, abstain from doing so. By holding him or speaking to him in an encouraging tone, you will be reinforcing his fear instead of lessening it. Likewise, if you yourself are afraid of storms, try to relax. Fear can be contagious. Some trainers believe that a fair number of dogs become scared of storms as a result of nothing more than their owners' adverse reactions to them.

For extreme cases of sound shyness, a natural over-the-counter sedative such as melatonin may be helpful. If you live in an area that is prone to severe storms, your veterinarian may be able to prescribe a tranquilizer to help your pet remain calm. Often, though, the dark clouds have usually passed before the medication has had a chance to get into the dog's system to do its work.

Separation Anxiety

Sometimes excessive barking is a sign of a more serious problem—separation anxiety. In addition to barking or howling, separation anxiety can further present itself in the form of chewing, housetraining regression, and sometimes even self-mutilation. One indication that you are dealing with an anxiety issue is if you offer your dog a treat when you leave and frequently return to see that it has remained uneaten.

The most common underlying causes of canine separation anxiety are confusion, fear, and stress. A variety of issues could be at the root of the problem. Perhaps your dog was taken from his mother too early, a common occurrence at puppy mills. Or your dog's separation anxiety may have developed as a result of being left at a shelter, leaving him especially fearful of your leaving him now. Maybe you have returned to working full time after taking a few weeks off to spend with your new dog. Again, this is a situation in which teaching basic obedience skills can help your dog become a more confident, less anxious being, which is the key to reversing this condition.

Spend time with your dog regularly. Take him for walks often; regular exercise can significantly reduce your dog's stress. If possible, provide your dog with a crate, and follow the protocol of slowing introducing him to it while you are at home. If you cannot seem to correct the problem, consider enrolling your dog in day care or having someone else care for him when you cannot be there. Even having a dog walker stop by midday may offer just enough of a break from the solitude to help him cope with being alone while you are away.

FINDING AN ANIMAL BEHAVIOR SPECIALIST

The work of an animal behaviorist involves observing, interpreting, and modifying animal behavior to help clients solve their pets' most serious problem behaviors. The biggest difference between behaviorists and other animal trainers or instructors is the severity of the problems they address. Dog trainers and obedience instructors help owners prevent negative behaviors before they become issues. They may also work with owners to correct mild problem behaviors. Behaviorists, on the other hand, deal with more substantial matters.

The advice of a behaviorist may be necessary if your dog suffers from acute anxiety or phobias, aggression, or other behavioral disorders. In most situations, conventional trainers are not qualified to deal with these issues. Even a veterinarian may not be able to help in many cases.

If your dog acts out most often when you are not home, he may be trying to tell you that he is bored or lonely.

Like dog trainers and obedience instructors, behaviorists do not need any form of licensing to do their work, so careful selection is a must. Although a certification process does exist, it is still fairly new and not well known; currently, only a limited number of certified behaviorists are available. You can find a directory of these individuals at www.animalbehavior.org. What is most important is that you are comfortable with the individual you choose, but you should also seek a person with a certain level of education and experience dealing with animals, particularly small dogs. A degree in some form of psychology or zoology is a definite advantage. The person should also possess dog training knowledge and experience. References from former clients are

good, but recommendations from veterinarians and humane societies are even better. If you cannot find a certified behaviorist in your area, these are the best resources to explore.

It is far easier to prevent an undesirable behavior than it is to correct it. This makes proactive training extremely important for adopted dogs. If you are faced with a few unpleasant behaviors from the beginning, don't procrastinate in dealing with them. By allowing your dog to behave inappropriately, you will only reinforce his negative behaviors.

WHEN THINGS DON'T WORK OUT

Sometimes an owner with the best of intentions can choose the wrong dog. If despite your best efforts things aren't working out, you must consider what is best for both you and your adopted dog. Some dogs bond with one family member but experience a strong dislike or resentment toward another. Other dogs can't seem to forge bonds with any of their owners. Perhaps you have realized that correcting your adopted dog's problem behaviors is beyond your training abilities, even with the help you have sought. Or maybe you realized after the adoption that your dog is a biter. If you are afraid of the dog or if you feel your frustration escalating to a point where you fear you could harm him, it may be best for you to relinquish him.

If you are unsure what you should do, discuss your situation with your veterinarian, a professional trainer, or a volunteer from the shelter or rescue. An objective third party may be able to help you identify a solution you hadn't considered. Certain breeds can take longer than others to connect with new people. For some dogs, a medical issue may be at the root of the problem. And very often owners have unrealistic timetables for their expectations. Bonding and training both take considerable time and patience.

If you decide that you cannot make the situation work, you must take the necessary steps to find the dog a more suitable home. If you adopted your dog through a breed rescue, do not surrender him to a shelter. As your agreement probably stipulates, you must give him back to the rescue organization. You may need to wait a short time (from a few days to a few weeks) for the volunteers to arrange for transportation and foster care. Try to be patient during this time. The rescue may be

For More Information

If your adopted dog suffers from separation anxiety, I highly recommend reading Patricia McConnell's book on the subject, entitled *I'll Be Home Soon: How to Prevent and Treat Separation Anxiety.*

handling multiple relinquishments simultaneously.

If you adopted your dog from a shelter and you didn't sign anything stating that you would return him to that facility in the event that you couldn't keep him, you may try to find the dog a home on your own. Ask your vet, your dog trainer, and even friends and family members to help you spread the word to anyone who might be interested in adopting the animal. This word-of-mouth method of finding a new adoptive owner is preferable to posting ads online or in the newspaper. If aggression is an issue, however, it may be best to return him to the shelter.

If you must resort to advertisement, never offer a dog for free. Ask the new owner to reimburse you for at least part of your original adoption fee. People tend to take dog ownership more seriously when they pay at least something for their pets. Even worse than those who adopt dogs because they are free, though, are those individuals who actually try to make money on the animals. As deplorable as it may seem, some people actually make a business out of answering free-to-good-home ads, and then selling the dogs to research laboratories, puppy mills, and even dog-fighting operations. The person you meet may seem like an upstanding citizen, parent, or animal lover, but this can all be part of the act.

Before transferring your dog to someone else's care, gather all his health records and any belongings that you have purchased for him such as toys or a bed. Having these latter items with him can make the transition easier on him. When you leave your adopted dog, be strong. Prolonging your exit with hugs and tearful goodbyes will only make the situation harder on both of you.

Finally, you must decide whether or not you will adopt another dog. I recommend waiting a while before making this immense decision. Even if you never bonded closely with your adopted dog, you will need some time to grieve the loss. The problem may have been a bad match between you and the dog you chose, or it may have been that you are not truly ready to own a dog at this time in your life. When and if you think you are ready for another pet, you also should take your time in selecting him so that you are certain that the next time around you will be able to commit to him for the rest of his life.

Finding Your Adopted Dog a New Home

If you choose to find a home for your pet yourself, follow these guidelines:

- Advertise through friends, neighbors, and local veterinarians first; then, if all else fails, try the newspaper. Your chances of finding your pet a good home are increased when you check references.

- Visit the prospective new home to get a feel for the environment in which your pet will be living. Explain that the pet is part of your family and that you want to make sure he will be cared for properly and that you want to see how the animal responds to the new home. Screen potential homes carefully.

- Don't be fooled. If anyone refuses to allow you to visit their home, do not place your pet with them. Individuals known as "bunchers" routinely answer free-to-good-home ads, posing as people who want family pets when, in actuality, they sell pets to animal dealers. Dogfighters have also been known to obtain domestic animals for baiting through free-to-good-home ads. These people are professionals who may even bring children or their mothers with them when picking up pets.

- Always be mindful of your own safety when you go to interview potential adopters or if you allow a prospective adopter to enter your home.

- Carefully consider all the elements of the new home: Will your pet get along with small children? Is the family planning to keep the dog chained outside as a watch dog? Does the family have a veterinary reference? Do not be shy about asking questions. Your pet's life and happiness may depend on it.

- Ask for a valid form of identification (preferably a driver's license). Record the number for your records, and require the new owner to sign a contract stating the requirements of adoption upon which both parties agree. As part of the contract, require the new owner to contact you if he or she decides at some point that they must give up the pet.

- Have your pet neutered or spayed before he goes to the new home. This will make the animal more adoptable and help stop irresponsible breeding.

- If your pet is chronically ill or has behavior problems, it may be difficult to find him a suitable home. A new owner may not be willing or able to deal with these issues, and it may also be difficult for the pet to adjust to a new home. The decision to humanely euthanize such a pet should not be made without thoughtful input from a veterinarian, a behaviorist, and the family, based on how well they believe the animal would adapt to a new home.

Finding a quality home for your pet can be a difficult and time-consuming process. Remember: Your local animal shelter has a qualified staff trained to screen and counsel adopters. Relinquishing your pet to your local shelter may be the best option for you and your pet.

(Courtesy of the Humane Society of the United States)

ACTIVITIES
With Your Adopted Dog

The best thing you can do for your adopted dog is to spend time with him regularly. Some activities involve getting together with other dog fanciers. You may compete in agility or obedience trials with your adopted dog, for instance. Other pastimes are more private. Many owners bring their dogs along for family picnics or hikes in the woods. Your idea of the perfect day may even be you, your dog, and peace and quiet in your own backyard. Whatever your preferences, you are sure to find an activity that both you and your new pet will find enjoyable. You may even discover several.

CANINE GOOD CITIZEN® PROGRAM

The Canine Good Citizen (CGC) program is a certification series begun by the American Kennel Club (AKC) in 1989. Stressing responsible pet ownership, the program rewards dogs who display good manners both at home and in the community. Although not mandatory, a CGC training program is offered to all owners and their dogs, and a certificate is awarded upon passing a ten-step test.

Uniting both dogs and owners with their communities through this program, the AKC requires owners to sign the *Responsible Dog Owners Pledge* before taking the test. This document states that the owner agrees to effectively provide for his or her dog for the rest of his life. It covers such important areas as health and safety, exercise and training, and basic quality of life. It even addresses such detailed issues as agreeing to clean up after your dog in public and never allowing him to infringe on the rights of others.

The test focuses on a dog's mastery of basic obedience skills and also his ability to interact peaceably with both human and canine strangers. A dog who passes this valuable examination is awarded an AKC certificate complete with the CGC logo embossed in gold. This certification can be useful to your dog in many other areas of advanced training.

Passing the Canine Good Citizen test is the mark of a well-behaved family pet.

Dogs of any age may participate in the CGC program, although puppies must be old enough to have had all necessary immunizations. The owners of younger dogs who pass the test are encouraged to have their dogs retested as adults as a means of ensuring that their temperaments and abilities have not changed during this formative period. All breeds and mixed breeds are welcome, as are older dogs. The AKC's Canine Good Citizen program has been an inspiration to many other countries around the world as they have developed their own CGC programs. To find a training class in your area, please contact your local AKC dog club.

THERAPY WORK

If you've ever had a pet before, you know the uncanny ability most animals possess to raise their owners' spirits even on their worst days. In my opinion, this is especially true of dogs. They don't judge you, they don't hold grudges, and they don't even notice if you look your absolute worst. They just want to be with you. By sharing something as seemingly simple as their company, they can lighten your load and make the stresses of everyday life seem just a little less important.

Therapy dogs take this natural gift a step further. In addition to offering their therapeutic companionship to their own beloved families, these animals, along with their thoughtful owners, share their time and love with other people who for various reasons can benefit from a similar lift. Visiting hospitals, nursing homes, and other places where individuals are facing difficult situations, therapy dogs make a difference by merely doing what they do best—being dogs.

I've always thought that the concept of bringing dogs and people together in this way was an admirable undertaking, but I once learned firsthand what a difference these dogs truly make when my father had been hospitalized. My mother and I were waiting for him to return to his room after a lengthy procedure when a retired couple arrived at the door with a gorgeous German Shepherd. They told us his name was Olbs von Huhnegrab—aka Max—and asked if we'd like him to visit with us. Because our minds were so affixed on my father and his illness, we said they were welcome to come in, but that the patient was not there at the moment. Of course, the couple immediately explained that Max was there to see everyone, patients and families alike.

At first I felt a little guilty petting this magnificent creature. I worried that I was taking up time he could be spending with patients who needed him much more than I did, but now I realize that his visit meant just as much to me as it did to anyone else that day. While talking to Max and his owners, my mother and I were able to relax just a little and focus our attention on something positive for the very first time that entire day. When they moved on to the next room, we felt more hopeful and were looking forward to telling my dad about the visit. The entire interaction lasted only minutes, but its effects helped carry us through the next two hours until my father finally returned from surgery.

Dogs with obedience training and strong social skills are good candidates for therapy work.

When most people think of working dogs, German Shepherds like Max often spring to mind. While this is certainly one of the most popular breeds utilized for many important jobs, therapy work (like many other canine vocations) is open to all breeds and breed mixes. Many adopted dogs can make excellent therapy dogs.

If you think your dog may have what it takes to become a therapy dog, you will need to have your dog certified before you are able to begin volunteering. Therapy Dogs

Celebrating Dogs of All Kinds

A great way for you and your adopted dog to help other animals in need of new homes is by participating in charity events that raise funds for adoption organizations in your area. Adopt-A-Dog's *Puttin' on the Dog Show* takes place annually in Greenwich, Connecticut. This for-fun dog show and community festival includes various canine competitions, vendors and food, a silent auction, and dogs available for adoption.

If you live on the opposite coast, the *Nuts for Mutts Dog Show and Pet Fair* in Woodland Hills, California, may be a fun way to kick off your summer. This show featuring mixed-breed dogs is judged by a panel of celebrity judges who award fun titles such as *Fastest Mutt, Most Ear-isistible Ears,* and *Most Toy/Ball Crazy.* These winners then compete for the prestigious top honor of *Best in Show.*

Communities across the country hold a multitude of similar fundraisers. The SPCA of Texas holds an annual *Strut Your Mutt* event, a 3-kilometer (2-mile) walk and fun run for dogs and their owners. The Humane Society of Greater Dayton in Ohio holds an annual 5-kilometer (3-mile) walk called the *Furry Skurry.* The Oregon Humane Society's annual *Doggy Dash* features a 3-kilometer (2-mile) walk followed by food, music, and doggy talent contests. Fun events like these increase awareness about the plight of homeless animals, and they provide both you and your pet with excellent opportunities for exercise and socialization—all while raising money for a deeply worthwhile cause. For a list of events like these in your area, contact your local humane society.

International, Inc. (TDI), which was founded in 1976, certifies, insures, and registers therapy dogs so that they may visit healthcare facilities. The first requirement of TDI is certification as a Canine Good Citizen. Although this will not ensure your dog a place in a therapy program, the social skills necessary for this achievement are an excellent indicator that a dog is a good candidate for therapy work. If your dog fails his CGC test the first time around, don't despair; he can still go on to take it again. Dogs who are poorly suited for this activity are usually red-flagged fairly quickly, but it may take a bit more time to make sure that other applicants are indeed the right dogs for the job, so try to be as patient as possible.

You may find that your dog has an affinity for a certain part of the population. Maybe he seems to particularly enjoy the company of children, senior citizens, or mentally disabled people. If this is the case, I strongly recommend indulging this fascination because members of these groups will likely mirror your dog's inexplicable rapport with them. Therapy work is about making people feel good, but your dog will also be enriched by the lives he touches through this noble activity.

OBEDIENCE

For many dog owners, advanced training in obedience begins with a relatively casual level of involvement, such as taking their dog to a basic obedience class. You may decide to check out competitive obedience training after working with your dog privately to teach him a few commands you think he should know. In many cases, though, both dog and owner discover that this seemingly stoic style of training can actually be a really fun pastime for all involved. Advanced obedience training, when properly implemented, is simply higher education for your dog.

In obedience competition, the first class you will enter is the novice class, also called the Companion Dog (CD) class. This beginning level focuses on demonstrating the skills of a good canine companion—heeling both on and off the leash at different speeds, coming when called, and staying for fixed periods of time while also remaining still and quiet with a group of other dogs. Your dog will also be required to stand for a basic physical examination by judges.

Next comes the open class. This second tier of obedience is called the Companion Dog Excellent (CDX) class. At this level, your dog will need to repeat many of the same exercises from the novice level, but off his leash and for longer periods of time. Jumping and retrieving tasks are also included in this phase.

The utility level, which provides your dog with a Utility Dog (UD) title, is for dogs nearing the top of their obedience game. At this stage, your dog will need to perform more difficult exercises, complete with hand signals, as well as scent

Obedience training is a great foundation for many other canine activities.

discrimination tasks. Once your dog can perform at this level, he can then go on to pursue the highest possible titles of Obedience Trial Champion (OTCh) and Utility Dog Excellent (UDX). Both are very prestigious titles and not easily or quickly achieved.

Like the CGC program, obedience is considered by many dog owners to be a great foundation for many other canine activities. Maybe your ultimate plan is for your dog to become a therapy dog, or perhaps you just want to participate in a fun weekend pastime together, with any awards being just an added bonus. No matter what obedience means to you and your dog, bear in mind that succeeding does not mean that your dog must earn all available titles. As with any activity, there is nothing wrong with striving toward your next goal, but the most important thing is enjoying the road that leads there. Any owner of a dog who earns a CDX or UD title should be very proud because these are very distinguished accomplishments.

CANINE SPORTS

Many dog owners enjoy being as active as their athletic pets. Canine sports offer these dog owners the opportunity to share in both the fun and exercise of advanced training activities. If you've never led an energetic dog around an agility course, you simply don't know what you are missing. Like trying new things? Consider trying flyball or canine freestyle with your dog. These canine sports are much more entertaining than sitting through a spinning class, and what's more, they allow you to spend fun time with your best friend.

Agility

An excellent opportunity for combining exercise and mental stimulation, agility is a truly interactive sport. Although it has only been recognized in the United States since 1994, it was actually developed in England in the 1970s. Resembling equestrian jumping competitions, canine agility courses consist of similar obstacles, but they are built to a smaller scale.

One thing that certainly isn't downsized, however, is the fun. Agility competitions have quickly become an amazingly popular pastime in this country for both participants and a mass of mesmerized onlookers. As handlers run alongside their dogs, the canine athletes make their way over colorful bars, vaulted walks, and seesaws. Keep watching, and you will see the same dogs dash through A-frames, suspended tires, and tunnels. Handlers may assist their pups by offering hand signals, verbal commands, or both.

If your energetic adopted puppy seems destined for this activity, you may have a few months to attend some events and work with your dog informally before making a final decision. Unlike obedience competition, a dog must be 12 months old to compete in agility. Although dogs must be physically fit for either activity, agility is considerably more strenuous on your dog's body than obedience. Because a puppy's growing bones and ligaments are weaker than an adult's, the potential for injury is lessened substantially by waiting this reasonable amount of time.

You can, of course, start introducing your dog to agility obstacles at any age. Encouraging a young dog to run through chutes or tunnels, for instance, may very well help him avoid any fears of these objects later. Do avoid any tasks involving jumping, though, until your dog is older. If you would like to at least familiarize your puppy with bar jumps, you may simply lay one bar on the ground and have your dog walk over it instead of jumping over it.

Agility is a sport in which a dog must navigate a timed obstacle course.

All dog breeds and mixed breeds are welcome to participate in agility. This is ultimately where the similarities of agility and obedience end, though. One distinctive difference that many agility enthusiasts tout as an advantage of their pastime is the amount of handler involvement allowed in this sport. Agility handlers are permitted to talk to their dogs, redirect

them verbally, or cheer them on at any time.

Every activity has both advantages as well as disadvantages. In the case of agility, the biggest drawbacks are the cost of setup and the space required for the multiple pieces of equipment. It can also be relatively time consuming to assemble a backyard course for practice, especially if you need to disassemble it when you are finished so that the space can be used for something else.

In some areas, owners who don't have the resources to practice the sport at home can rent entire agility rings by the hour or the day. At first, you can use certain makeshift items in place of more expensive equipment. For example, a home extension ladder can help teach a dog to walk within a narrow space or train him to focus his attention forward. Once you have determined that your dog is well suited to agility, you should then make a point of transitioning to conventional equipment so that your dog can acclimate to any subtle changes that could make a difference in his future performance in the ring. Any item you use should also be completely safe for your dog.

Once ready for competition, your dog will be entered in the novice class. Succeeding at this level will earn him a Novice Agility Dog (NAD) title. Subsequent titles are then available in the following order: Open Agility Dog (OAD), Agility Dog Excellent (ADX), and Master Agility Excellent (MAX). To obtain each title, a dog must earn a

Deciding Which Activity to Choose

How do you know which activity your adopted dog would enjoy the most? Ask him! Of course, he won't be able to articulate his answer through words, but he will surely demonstrate a love (or distaste) for a particular activity once he is exposed to it a few times. When my son started school, my husband and I exposed him to a new sport each season. In the fall, we signed him up for soccer. In the winter, it was basketball. Summer led us to tee-ball. By the time he reached the second grade, we knew baseball was a thing of the past for him, but he seemed to enjoy soccer immensely. He now plays this sport both indoors and outdoors throughout the year. You can likely find your dog's passion this same way.

You can get a feel for your dog's potential in obedience, for instance, by attending a basic class with him. Likewise, you may be able to assess your dog's interest in agility by taking him to events where other dogs are competing. Occasionally, a dog may excel at more than one organized activity, but more often a dog gravitates toward a specific pastime. Limiting your dog's involvement in organized activities to just one or two types can also prevent him from becoming overscheduled. Not unlike a child, your dog should always approach his extracurricular activities with enthusiasm. Making time off a regular part of his schedule will help maintain his interest when it's time to head back into the ring.

qualifying score in the respective class on three separate occasions and from two different judges. Issuance of the MAX title is dependent upon 10 qualifying scores in the Agility Excellent Class.

Flyball

Flyball is an exciting canine sport that requires both speed and dexterity. Upon hearing a signal, the dog's owner releases him on the flyball course, a small and straight strip of land. His goal is to run over four hurdles to the end of this course, where a box with a trap and foot lever awaits him. The dog jumps onto the foot lever, releasing a tennis ball into the air. After he has leapt to catch this ball, he then darts back to his owner with the ball. This is all timed down to the second. Typically, flyball is a team sport consisting of two to four relay teams of four dogs per team. Dogs may compete on either single-breed or multi-breed teams.

Flyball is a particularly fun pastime for dogs ready to take regular ball playing to the next level. A great number of dogs competing in flyball are members of the herding group, but all breeds and mixed breeds are allowed to play on multi-breed teams. Although larger dogs tend to dominate in this sport, smaller breeds are welcomed onto multi-breed teams with great enthusiasm because the height of the hurdles is set according to the height of the smallest dog on the team. Little dogs also often clock impressive times, despite the fact that they need to use much more of their physical power to trigger the ball release.

Canine Freestyle

If you and your dog enjoy moving around to music, canine freestyle may be just the sport to provide both of you with a fun opportunity for exercise and entertainment. Led by the World Canine Freestyle Organization (WCFO), this sport is relatively new, but it has been catching on all over the world for the last couple of decades. Two basic varieties of freestyle exist: musical freestyle and heelwork-to-music. The former version consists of carefully choreographed music programs in which both the owner and dog dance together. It involves intense teamwork, athleticism, and even costumes for both participants. The latter version incorporates traditional canine obedience skills into the

If you and your dog enjoy moving around to music, canine freestyle may be just the sport to provide both of you with a fun opportunity for exercise and entertainment.

routine. Both require an intense level of creativity and a willingness to let loose and have fun.

Although freestyle is very much a form of individual artistic expression, rules dictate what is and isn't allowed in competition. Likewise, a very specific point system is followed for judging. A 35-page list of these guidelines is available at the WCFO website at www.worldcaninefreestyle.org.

Freestyle is truly an event for the whole family. An owner may compete in canine freestyle with either one or two dogs. Two people may compete together with their canine duo in a pairs event, or participants may compete together in teams of three or more people and an equal number of dogs. There is also a junior division for kids under 18 years of age and dogs under 6 months, as well as a senior division for people 65 and older and dogs 9 years and up. There is even a division for mentally and/or physically handicapped dogs and their owners who also may be mentally challenged.

The best way to learn about canine freestyle is by attending an event. Many offer instruction workshops for those interested in becoming involved in this fun new sport.

Like the recent inclusion of ice dancing in the winter Olympics, acceptance of canine freestyle as a bona fide sport among dog enthusiasts is still in its early stages. Many owners who prefer more traditional sports such as flyball or agility may scoff at dogs and owners jitter-bugging their way across the dance ring, but it's clearly those participants who are having the most fun. Watching a freestyle competition can be great fun for onlookers as well. You will be truly amazed at what some of these dogs and their owners can do.

COMPETING IN MULTIPLE EVENTS

Can your adopted dog compete in more than one advanced

activity? The short answer is yes. No rules state that a canine freestyle contestant cannot compete in obedience, or that an obedience competitor cannot participate in agility. Many dogs participate in two or more advanced training activities without a problem. Some dogs, along with their owners, thrive on involvement in a variety of challenging activities.

Others insist that, many times, one activity can interfere with or limit a dog's success in another. A dog who has gone through a painstaking process to achieve titles in obedience, for instance, may have a hard time adapting to the innate freedoms of agility. Another dog with a similar past could take to agility quite well, but regress in his mastery of obedience, while yet another may succeed in both activities equally well.

If you think you both might enjoy a new activity, try it. You are always free to take a break from one activity and then come back to it if a new one ends up not being right for you and your dog. The most important thing is that both of you are having fun. Do be careful, though, not to over-schedule either yourself or your dog. These activities, while serious in nature, are meant to be enjoyable. If they start feeling like obligations, or if your dog seems to be losing his fondness for them, it may be time to think about reducing the number of events you attend regularly.

Keeping Your Dog Hydrated

Just like human athletes, dogs need to drink plenty of water when competing in sports of any kind. It can be easier to remember to bring along some water for your dog when the weather is hot, but you also must be sure to keep your dog hydrated at indoor events or those held in the winter. Some companies have even begun selling sports drinks for pets formulated to replenish the electrolytes they lose during active play. Whichever you choose, remember to bring along a bowl for your pet. Collapsible versions are available at most pet supply stores.

ONE-ON-ONE ACTIVITIES WITH YOUR ADOPTED DOG

Activities need not be organized or competitive to be fun for you and your pet. Getting out together—just the two of you—is another great way of giving your dog exercise and a change of scenery, as well as creating important bonding time with you. Involving your dog in some of the pastimes you already find rewarding can make these pursuits even more meaningful and enjoyable for you as well.

If your family is heading for an outdoor event or day trip, take your dog along. Where I live near the coast of Maine, a ferry takes passengers out to the various islands around Casco Bay and back to the mainland several times each day. As long as they are leashed, dogs are welcome to board the ferry to tag along with their seafaring owners. You don't have to leave land, though, to include your dog in your plans. Picnic at a local park, or have lunch at a restaurant with outdoor tables. State parks are often great places to bring pets, provided that dogs are allowed. Some wonderful books have been written to detail the best dog-friendly places in various locations around the United States. Check your local library or online for such locations where you live.

Hiking and Running

Walking and running are two of the healthiest forms of exercise for both people and dogs. What's more, taking part requires no fancy equipment or major expense. You can enjoy either activity virtually anywhere, anytime. When your dog walks or runs, his body utilizes and strengthens various muscles, and he experiences an increase in heart rate, a basic requirement of any cardiovascular activity. Sensible precautions must be taken with either pastime, though, to help prevent the dangers of physical injury, overexertion, and dehydration.

Activities need not be organized or competitive to be fun for you and your pet. Spending time walking or playing a game of fetch with your dog can be just as rewarding.

Walking can serve as a sensible introduction to a more intense exercise program, such as running, or it can be a worthwhile activity in its own right. Ideal for dogs of virtually all fitness levels, walking strikes many people as the quintessential human–canine pastime. It requires no instruction, it provides both dogs and owners with a regular dose of fresh air and sunshine, and it can be adjusted to fit into almost any routine.

Running (or jogging) with your adopted dog, on the other hand, is an activity that demands a bit more preparation and a lot more vigilance. A dog who has never before run for any length of time, for example, needs to be introduced to the pursuit gradually, starting with only very short distances in the beginning and

progressively increasing them. Just because your dog can run around with you in the backyard for what seems like hours on end does not mean he can keep up with you on a genuine 5-mile (8-km) run with no practical experience.

Always be on the lookout for signs that your dog needs a break. These can range from subtle (panting excessively and slowing down) to more obvious (increased salivation and outright stopping to sit down) indicators. If your dog tells you he needs to rest, honor his request by finding the nearest patch of shade for a respite period. Never run without taking along water for both you and your dog.

If your dog is overweight, you should discuss the prospect of running together with your veterinarian, who may likely suggest postponing vigorous exercise until his weight is down to a more reasonable level. In the meantime, grab your dog's leash, don your walking shoes, and get on the road to better health by putting one foot in front of the other.

Settling Upset Tummies

If your dog gets motion sickness, try giving him a little crystallized ginger or a couple of gingersnap cookies. This tasty home remedy is surprisingly effective.

Games

Some owners prefer to train and exercise their dogs in less structured settings, perhaps at home in their backyards. This more relaxed approach can serve as a basis for more conventional training down the road or be used for nothing more than pure fun. By observing your adopted dog during this kind of play, you can also gain much insight into his learning style and potential for different activities. A dog who likes to run and jump may be well suited for agility, whereas a dog who seems to look to you for direction during play may be an excellent candidate for obedience.

The best thing about all these activities is that you are not required to continue up a ladder of success. A friend of mine has a very intelligent dog who especially enjoys the tunnels in agility, but shows no interest in any of the other obstacles. Agility competitions are not for this animal, but she still has a load of fun streaming through the vivid nylon passageways in her own backyard nonetheless. Listening to the cues your dog gives you about what he most likes and dislikes is one of the best things you can do to meet his needs and create rewarding pastimes for you both.

When dogs are given an adequate amount of recreation time, they are healthier, happier, and better behaved.

Playing Ball

Many dogs enjoy playing ball, and most adopted dogs are no exception. Make sure your dog's ball is the right size for his mouth. A smaller dog will have trouble picking up a large ball, and a bigger pet can choke on a tiny ball. The best way to play ball with a smaller pet is by bouncing the ball gently away from the dog and allowing him to run after it, or by rolling the ball slowly toward him. If your dog is larger and athletic, you may consider investing in a ball with a throwing wand. This long, spoon-like item helps owners throw the ball greater distances.

Fetch

Fetch is a game that can be played with any toy your adopted dog fancies. Keep in mind, however, that your dog might not be especially keen on giving up a particularly treasured item once he has taken possession of it. This can be part of the fun for your dog, but discontinue play if his possessiveness escalates to aggressive behavior.

Follow the Leader

Many dogs are naturals at playing follow the leader. Using various kinds of impromptu obstacles, this game can easily be played in a backyard or inside the home using furniture, hallways, and other items within your home as props. Placing a reward, such as a favorite toy or other treat, at the end of the course can be a fun addition.

Hide and Seek

Playing hide and seek is a great way to practice the *sit, stay,* and *come* commands with your dog. After giving the first two commands, find a place to hide and then call your dog. Remember to reward him for finding you. You can also hide a treat for your dog to find. As your dog becomes more and more adept at locating the treat, try hiding additional treats, which will lay the groundwork for a treasure hunt.

Playing Chase

One of the biggest mistakes an owner can make is chasing his or her dog during play. By doing so you are essentially teaching your dog to run away from you. This does not mean you must decline if your dog initiates a thrilling game of chase. Just make sure that you are always the one being chased and that the game remains playful and fun. Through well-planned playtime, you will be training your dog to always follow you.

Playing With Toys

Finally, don't forget toys! Toys can be a great motivator to get your dog moving. Saving one or two special items for more active playtimes can help ensure that your dog will be willing to participate in a good old-fashioned game of fetch when the time comes. Toys are also great nonedible rewards to use at the end of an informal training session.

Believe it or not, some dogs can be taught to pick up and put away their own toys. A variation of playing fetch, this game of sorts can be a fun and useful way to cap off each play session. Like many other games, it can alo be a great foundation for further training activities.

ESTABLISH A PLAYTIME ROUTINE

Seize the opportunity for play whenever your schedule allows. You don't need big chunks of time! Your dog will actually get more out of several shorter periods of play throughout the day than he will from one longer, exhausting session.

As with more organized activities, it is best to end games on a positive note. If you quit playing while your dog is still having fun, he will be more interested in joining in the fun the next time. This will help maintain his attention if you do wish to incorporate training into future playtimes.

Playtime, whether organized or spontaneous, can be a great stress reliever for both you and your new pet. When dogs are given an adequate amount of recreation time, they are healthier, happier, and better behaved. I can't think of a better habit to adopt than regular playtime with your beloved pet.

Give Your Dog the Runaround

Exercise is not only important for keeping your dog healthy, but it also plays a key role in creating a well-adjusted, well-behaved pet. A dog who gets regular exercise is tired at the end of the day—too tired to get into mischief. Being active also keeps your dog happy. Just as with people, dogs feel good when they exercise because of all the endorphins their bodies release in the process.

ASSOCIATIONS AND ORGANIZATIONS

RESOURCES

BREED CLUBS

American Kennel Club (AKC)
5580 Centerview Drive
Raleigh, NC 27606
Telephone: (919) 233-9767
Fax: (919) 233-3627
E-mail: info@akc.org
www.akc.org

Canadian Kennel Club (CKC)
89 Skyway Avenue, Suite 100
Etobicoke, Ontario M9W 6R4
Telephone: (416) 675-5511
Fax: (416) 675-6506
E-mail: information@ckc.ca
www.ckc.ca

Federation Cynologique Internationale (FCI)
Secretariat General de la FCI
Place Albert 1er, 13
B – 6530 Thuin
Belqique
www.fci.be

The Kennel Club
1 Clarges Street
London
W1J 8AB England
Telephone: 0870 606 6750
Fax: 0207 518 1058
www.the-kennel-club.org.uk

United Kennel Club (UKC)
100 E. Kilgore Road
Kalamazoo, MI 49002-5584
Telephone: (269) 343-9020
Fax: (269) 343-7037
E-mail: pbicell
@ukcdogs.com
www.ukcdogs.com

PET SITTERS

National Association of Professional Pet Sitters
15000 Commerce Parkway, Suite C
Mt. Laurel, New Jersey 08054
Telephone: (856) 439-0324
Fax: (856) 439-0525
E-mail: napps@ahint.com
www.petsitters.org

Pet Sitters International
201 East King Street
King, NC 27021-9161
Telephone: (336) 983-9222
Fax: (336) 983-5266
E-mail: info@petsit.com
www.petsit.com

RESCUE ORGANIZATIONS AND ANIMAL WELFARE GROUPS

American Humane Association (AHA)
63 Inverness Drive East
Englewood, CO 80112
Telephone: (303) 792-9900
Fax: (303) 792-5333
www.americanhumane.org

American Society for the Prevention of Cruelty to Animals (ASPCA)
424 E. 92nd Street
New York, NY 10128-6804
Telephone: (212) 876-7700
www.aspca.org

Royal Society for the Prevention of Cruelty to Animals (RSPCA)
Telephone: 0870 3335 999
Fax: 0870 7530 284
www.rspca.org.uk

The Humane Society of the United States (HSUS)
2100 L Street, NW
Washington DC 20037
Telephone: (202) 452-1100
www.hsus.org

SPORTS

Canine Freestyle Federation, Inc.
Secretary: Brandy Clymire
E-mail: secretary@canine-freestyle.org
www.canine-freestyle.org

International Agility Link (IAL)
Global Administrator:
Steve Drinkwater
E-mail: yunde@powerup.au
www.agilityclick.com/~ial

North American Dog Agility Council
11522 South Hwy 3
Cataldo, ID 83810
www.nadac.com

North American Flyball Association
www.flyball.org
1400 West Devon Avenue #512
Chicago, IL 6066
Telephone: (800) 318-6312

United States Dog Agility Association
P.O. Box 850955
Richardson, TX 75085-0955
Telephone: (972) 487-2200
www.usdaa.com

World Canine Freestyle Organization
P.O. Box 350122
Brooklyn, NY 11235-2525
Telephone: (718) 332-8336
www.worldcaninefreestyle.org

THERAPY

Delta Society
875 124th Ave NE, Suite 101
Bellevue, WA 98005
Telephone: (425) 226-7357
Fax: (425) 235-1076
E-mail: info@deltasociety.org
www.deltasociety.org

Therapy Dogs Incorporated
PO Box 5868
Cheyenne, WY 82003
Telephone: (877) 843-7364
E-mail: therdog@sisna.com
www.therapydogs.com

Therapy Dogs International (TDI)
88 Bartley Road
Flanders, NJ 07836
Telephone: (973) 252-9800
Fax: (973) 252-7171
E-mail: tdi@gti.net
www.tdi-dog.org

TRAINING

Animal Behavior Society
www.animalbehavior.org

Association of Pet Dog Trainers (APDT)
150 Executive Center Drive
Box 35
Greenville, SC 29615
Telephone: (800) PET-DOGS
Fax: (864) 331-0767
E-mail: information@apdt.com
www.apdt.com

National Association of Dog Obedience Instructors (NADOI)
PMB 369
729 Grapevine Hwy.
Hurst, TX 76054-2085
www.nadoi.org

VETERINARY AND HEALTH RESOURCES

Academy of Veterinary Homeopathy (AVH)
P.O. Box 9280
Wilmington, DE 19809
Telephone: (866) 652-1590
Fax: (866) 652-1590
E-mail: office@TheAVH.org
www.theavh.org

American Academy of Veterinary Acupuncture (AAVA)
100 Roscommon Drive
Suite 320
Middletown, CT 06457
Telephone: (860) 635-6300
Fax: (860) 635-6400
E-mail: office@aava.org
www.aava.org

American Animal Hospital Association (AAHA)
P.O. Box 150899
Denver, CO 80215-0899
Telephone: (303) 986-2800
Fax: (303) 986-1700
E-mail: info@aahanet.org
www.aahanet.org/index.cfm

American College of Veterinary Internal Medicine (ACVIM)
1997 Wadsworth Blvd.
Suite A
Lakewood, CO 80214-5293
Telephone: (800) 245-9081
Fax: (303) 231-0880
E-mail: ACVIM@ACVIM.org
www.acvim.org

American College of Veterinary Ophthalmologists (ACVO)
P.O. Box 1311
Meridian, Idaho 83860
Telephone: (208) 466-7624
Fax: (208) 466-7693
E-mail: office@acvo.com
www.acvo.com

American Holistic Veterinary Medical Association (AHVMA)
2218 Old Emmorton Road
Bel Air, MD 21015
Telephone: (410) 569-0795
Fax: (410) 569-2346
E-mail: office@ahvma.org
www.ahvma.org

American Veterinary Medical Association (AVMA)
1931 North Meacham Road
Suite 100
Schaumburg, IL 60173
Telephone: (847) 925-8070
Fax: (847) 925-1329
E-mail: avmainfo@avma.org
www.avma.org

ASPCA Animal Poison Control Center
1717 South Philo Road
Suite 36
Urbana, IL 61802
Telephone: (888) 426-4435
www.aspca.org

British Veterinary Association (BVA)
7 Mansfield Street
London
W1G 9NQ England
Telephone: 020 7636 6541
Fax: 020 7436 2970
E-mail: bvahq@bva.co.uk
www.bva.co.uk

Canine Eye Registration Foundation (CERF)
VMDB/CERF
1248 Lynn Hall
625 Harrison St.
Purdue University
West Lafayette, IN 47907-2026
Telephone: (765) 494-8179
E-mail: CERF@vmbd.org
www.vmdb.org

Orthopedic Foundation for Animals (OFA)
2300 NE Nifong Blvd
Columbus, Missouri 65201-3856
Telephone: (573) 442-0418
Fax: (573) 875-5073
E-mail: ofa@offa.org
www.offa.org

DEDICATION

This book is dedicated to all the people—shelter workers, rescue volunteers, and adoptive owners—who have taken the time to speak with me about their experiences with dog adoption. Each and every one of you is making an important difference.

ABOUT THE AUTHOR

Tammy Gagne is a freelance writer who specializes in the health and behavior of companion animals. In addition to being a regular contributor to several national pet care magazines, she has authored numerous books for both adults and children. She resides in northern New England with her husband, son, dogs, and parrots.

PHOTO CREDITS

James B. Adson (Sutterstock): 88; Poprujin Aleksey (Shutterstock): 43; Amy Chiara Allen (Shutterstock): 21; Galina Barskaya (Shutterstock): 36, 200; Vera Bogaerts (Shutterstock): 66; Paulette Braun (Shutterstock): 72, 159; Ariel Bravy (Shutterstock): 79; Joy Brown (Shutterstock): 105; Mindy W. M. Chung (Shutterstock): 182; Cynoclub (Shutterstock): 191; Lindsay Dean (Shutterstock): 145 Digitalsport-photoagency (Shutterstock): 147; Tim Elliot (Shutterstock): 99; Sonya Etchison (Shutterstock): 6, 34, 96, 141; Bryan Firestone (Shutterstock): 172; Fred Goldstein (Shutterstock): 162; Cindy Haggerty (Shutterstock): 114; Daniel Hebert (Shutterstock): 76; Nicole Hrustyk (Shutterstock): 126; IntraClique LLC (Shutterstock): 132; Iofoto (Shutterstock): 189; Judy Ben Joud (Shutterstock): 29, 58; Alister G. Jupp (Shutterstock): 60; Andreas Klute (Shutterstock): 31; maxstockphoto (Shutterstock): 166 Patrick McCall (Shutterstock): 161; Jean Morrison (Shutterstock): 152; Lev Olka (Shutterstock): 196; Bailey One (Shutterstock): 62 Lovesky Pavel (Shutterstock): 65; Kirk Peart Professional Imaging (Shutterstock): 71, 157; Mark William Penny (Shutterstock): 198 Michele Perbellini (Shutterstock): 128; photosbyjohn (Shutterstock): 92; Tina Rencelj (Shutterstock): 40, 177; Jack S (Shutterstock): 57 Jennifer Sekerka (Shutterstock): 47; Kristian Sekulic (Shutterstock): 55; Shutterstock: 68, 84, 95, 164, 186, ; Alan Smillie (Shutterstock): 11; Ljupco Smokovski (Shutterstock): 15, 139; Fernando Jose Vasconcelos Soares (Shutterstock): 17; Claudia Steininger (Shutterstock): 116; Gemmav D. Stokes (Shutterstock): 123; Mihhail Triboi (Shutterstock): 83; HTuller (Shutterstock): 73 vgm (Shutterstock): 193; Lynn Watson (Shutterstock): 22; Andrew Williams (Shutterstock): 18; Cindi Wilson (Shutterstock): 109; Robert Young (Shutterstock): 90

All other photos courtesy of Isabelle Francais, Eric Isselée, and TFH Archives
Cover photo: Robert Young (Shutterstock)
Back cover photos: Dwight Lyman (Shutterstock), Sonya Etchison (Shutterstock)

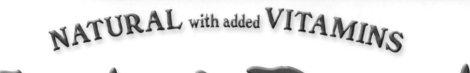